Abdessalam Benabdelali is a professor in the Faculty of Letters at Mohammed V University in Rabat, Morocco, and editor-in-chief of *Pensée et Critique*. His notable works include *Political Philosophy of Al-Farabi* and *The Mythology of Reality, between Connection and Separation.*

Marouane Zakhir is an associate professor of English at Chouaib Doukkali University in El-Jadida Morocco, where he is also an active member of the Applied Language and Culture Studies Research Lab.

Christian Hawkey is a poet, translator and educator. He has written several full-length poetry collections, including *Sift*, as well as the widely celebrated genre-defying book *Ventrakl*. He lives in Berlin, Germany.

Gayatri Chakravorty Spivak is University Professor in the Humanities at Columbia University. She is the author of *A Critique of Postcolonial Reason* (1999) and other works.

Hosam Aboul-Ela is a professor of English at University of Houston, Texas. He is the author of *Other South: Faulkner, Coloniality, and the Mariategui Tradition* (2007) and *Domestications: American Empire, Literary Culture, and the Postcolonial Lens* (2018).

ABDESSALAM BENABDELALI
Writings on Translation

TRANSLATED BY MAROUANE ZAKHIR
AND CHRISTIAN HAWKEY

SERIES INTRODUCTION BY
GAYATRI CHAKRAVORTY SPIVAK

LONDON NEW YORK CALCUTTA

ELSEWHERE TEXTS

Series Editors: Gayatri Chakravorty Spivak and Hosam Aboul-Ela

Seagull Books, 2025

First published in Arabic asE
Kitābāt fī al-Tarjama

First published in English translation by Seagull Books, 2025

Paperback ISBN 978 1 80309 511 0

Hardback ISBN 978 1 80309 510 3

British Library Cataloguing-in-Publication Data

A catalogue record for this book is available from the British Library

Typeset by Seagull Books, Calcutta, India

Contents

ELSEWHERE TEXTS

A General Introduction

'Theory' is an English transcription of the Greek *theorein*. Corresponding words exist in the major European languages. Our series Elsewhere Texts works within these limits. 'Theory' has been creolized into innumerable languages. Yet the phenomenon of 'seeing or making visible correctly'—the meaning in Greek that will still suffice—does not necessarily relate to that word—'theory'—in those languages. This describes the task of the editors of a translated series on theory in the world. How does 'theory' look elsewhere from the Euro-US? Since our texts are modern, there is often at least an implicit awareness that 'proper' theory looks different as the 'same' theory elsewhere.

Heidegger thought that truth is destined to be thought by the man of 'Western Europe'.[1] Our series does not offer a legitimizing counter-essentialism. Take a look at the map and see how tiny Europe is—not even really a continent—but, as Derrida would say, a cap, a headland.[2] Such a tiny place, yet who can deny Derrida's description, which is an historical and empirical observation? Look at the tables of contents of the most popular UK/US critical anthologies, and you will see corroboration of the essentialist conviction that goes with the historical claim. The counter-essentialism is reflected in the choice of critics from 'the rest of the world', and today's espousal of 'the Global South'. Just being non-white is the counter-essence. The colour line, an axiomatics for the other side, as Black Lives Matter points out.

The influential *Norton Anthology of Theory and Criticism*, for example, lets in only Maimonides before the modern university system kicks in.[3] But

---

1 Martin Heidegger, *What Is Called Thinking*? (Fred D. Wieck and J. Glenn Gray trans) (New York: Harper and Row, 1968).

2 Jacques Derrida, *The Other Heading* (Pascale-Anne Brault and Michael B. Naas trans) (Bloomington: Indiana University Press, 1992).

3 Vincent B. Leitch (ed.), *The Norton Anthology of Theory and Criticism* (New York: Norton, 2010). I have to tell my reader that I called my father 'Maimonides' because he was born in Mymensingh in what is now Bangladesh! Comparative Literature!

even if they had let in Khaled Ziadeh, Marta Lamas and Marilena Chaui, the material would have been determined by the epistemological procedures of that system.[4] Norton lets in W. E. B Du Bois, the first African-American to get a doctorate from Harvard, the man who felt that 'of the greatest importance was the opportunity which my *Wanderjahre* [wandering years] in Europe gave of looking at the world as a man and not simply from a narrow racial and provincial outlook'.[5] Du Bois emphatically claimed that the African American was the best example of the subject of the Declaration of Independence (the Founding Fathers were standing in). It is therefore significant that he claims here to inhabit the persona of Wilhelm Meister, Goethe's hero, with the trajectory not fully reversed. Meister came to the United States to act out the European Enlightenment in this new land—a trip described in Goethe's *Wilhelm Meisters Wanderjahre* (Wilhelm Meister's Journeyman Years)—a hope which Du Bois nuanced, perhaps as soon as his scholarship to the Friedrich Wilhelm University from the Slater Fund for the Education of Freedmen was cancelled, the year after President Hayes' death, by a Standing Committee on Education chaired by a former Lieutenant Colonel in the Confederate Army, the army that had fought to retain slavery and the slave trade in the US Civil War. (Hayes himself destroyed the possibility of Reconstruction by the 1877 Compromise with the Southern Democrats in order to retain the Presidency of the United States.) Du Bois as a young man was critical of his racism but probably not aware of political details, as he was later.

In the *Norton Anthology*, we get Zora Neale Hurston (Columbia), Langston Hughes (Harlem Renaissance via Columbia), Frantz Fanon (University of Lyon), Chinua Achebe (University College, Ibadan; professor in the US), Stuart Hall (Oxford), Ngugi wa Thiong'o (Leeds; professor in the US), Taban Lo Liyong (Iowa), Henry Owuwor Anyuumba (Iowa), Spivak (Cornell), Houston Baker (UCLA), Gloria Anzaldua (UCSC), Homi Bhabha (Oxford), Barbara Christian (Columbia), Barbara Smith (Mount Holyoke),

---

4 These authors were published by Palgrave in a series similar to this one, under the same editorial collaboration.

5 Cited in Henry Louis Gates, Jr., 'The Black Letters on the Sign: W. E. B. Du Bois and the Canon' in *The Oxford W. E. B. Du Bois* (New York: Oxford University Press, 2007), VOL. 8, p. *xvi*.

Henry Louis Gates, Jr. (Cambridge), bell hooks (UCSC). The point I am making is not that these writers have not challenged Eurocentrism. It is that they are sabotaging it from within, and this is a historical fact that must be turned around so that there is a chance for widening the circle. Fanon stands out because he is the only one who clearly operated outside the Euro–US, though he was what Du Bois would call a Black European, literally fighting Europe, also from within, located in a geographical exterior. Yet one cannot help suspecting that the certificate of violence granted him by the French philosopher Jean-Paul Sartre (in the Introduction to Fanon's last book *The Wretched of the Earth*) had a hand in this.

(In the next most influential anthology, the rest-of-the world entries are almost identical, but for Audre Lorde [Columbia], Geraldine Heng [Cornell], Ania Loomba [Sussex], Chidi Okonkwo [University of Auckland], Jamaica Kincaid [Franconia and New School].[6] Again, Fanon is the only working 'outsider'. I am sure the general pattern is repeated everywhere. I have myself been so tokenized through my long work life as representing 'Third World criticism', that I am particularly alive to the problem.)[7]

Our position is against a rest-of-the-world counter-essentialism, which honours the history-versus-tradition binary opposition. We recognize that a hegemonic Euro-US series can only access work abroad that is continuous with Euro-US radicalism.[8] To open ourselves to what lies beyond is another kind of effort. Within the limits of our chosen task we focus, then, on another phenomenon.

---

6 Michael Ryan and Julie Rivkin, *Literary Theory: An Anthology* (Malden: Wiley Blackwell, 2004).

7 An example that has stayed with me over the years remains Diane Bell's excellent *Daughters of the Dreaming* (Minneapolis: University of Minnesota Press, 1993), which, in response to requests for inclusion of third-world material, put in Trin-ti Min-Ha and me, longtime faculty persons in prestigious United States universities!

8 This continuity and the discontinuous are beautifully staged in *Bamako* (2006) by Abderrahmane Sissako. Jean François Lyotard gave a clear articulation of the problem of discontinuity in *The Differend: Phrases in Dispute* (Georges Van den Abbeele trans.) (Minneapolis: University of Minnesota Press, 1988).

The history of the last few centuries has produced patterns of bi-lateral resistance. The formation is typically my nation-state, my region, my cultural formation over against 'the West'. These days there are global efforts at conferences, events and organizations that typically take the form of the Euro-US at the centre and a whole collection of 'other cultures', who connect through the imperial languages, protected by a combination of sanctioned ignorance and superficial solidarities, ignoring the internal problems when they are at these global functions.[9] The model is the fact and discipline of preservation. By the Nara document of 1994, it was insisted that preservation should be not only of built space but also of intangible cultural heritage. What started was the model that I have described above. It is now a tremendous capital-intensive fact of our world.

In and through our series, we want to combat this tendency. We want not only to present texts from different national origins to the US readership, but we want also to point out how each is singular in the philosophical sense, namely universalizable, though never universal. We are not working for area studies niche-marketing, though the work is always of specialist quality. In the interest of creating a diversified collectivity outside of the English readership, a long-term feature might be periodic conferences bringing the authors together.

The story begins for me in a conversation with the Subaltern Studies collective in 1986—asking them if I could arrange the publication of a selection from their work—because they were not available in the United States. A long-term preoccupation, then. To this was added Hosam Aboul-Ela's 2007 consolidation of a thought that was growing inside me: from the rest of the world, literary editors wanted fiction, poetry, drama—raw material. Theory came generally from 'us'. Seagull Books, the only publishing house based in South Asia with direct world distribution, and, unlike most Western conglomerates, uninterested in translations of theory not recognizable by the Eurocentric 'cosmopolitan' model, seems now the appropriate publisher.

9 My most memorable experience was to encounter a Maori activist-bookseller and an Indian feminist at such a convention, who had never heard of Frederick Douglass, where only in response to my questions did the South African participant admit to political problems with translation between indigenous languages, and the mainland Chinese participant to the barrier between Mandarin and Cantonese. Examples can be multiplied.

In the intervening three decades a small difference has imposed itself—the one I have been emphasizing so far—the justification for 'elsewhere'. Earlier I had felt that my brief within the profession was to share and show that the work overseas was really 'theoretical' by Western sizing. (I use the word 'size' here in the sense of *pointure* in Derrida.)[10] Hence, 'strategic use of essentialism'. Now I also feel the reader must learn that 'theory' need not look the same everywhere, that, for the independent mind, too much training in producing the European model in stylistic detail might be a hindrance. In my teacher training work in rural India, it is the illiterate man who understands things best because his considerable intelligence has not been hobbled by bad education or gender oppression. The lesson here is not that everyone should be illiterate, but that strong minds should not be ruined by bad education or imperatives to imitate.

The caution would apply to *Neighbourhood and Boulevard* by Khaled Ziadeh (belonging to our earlier series, see note 4)—not bad education, obviously, but the imperative to imitate 'French Theory'.[11] Ziadeh, in spite of his time at the Sorbonne, was not tempted. He theorizes by space and repetition; Hosam Aboul-Ela's Introduction to that book walks us through it. There are plenty of people writing in Arabic who produce work competitive with the best in European-style 'theory'. Reading Ziadeh, as Aboul-Ela points out, we have to learn to recognize 'theory' in another guise. My own work profits from his account of thc de-Ottomanization of the city by the French into an 'Islamic' space; because I think de-Ottomanization, still active in our time, has a history as old as the Fall of Constantinople, and, re-territorialized, backward into Byzantium. Today's Khilafat movement can be read as an example of how imperial historical violence can produce a counter-violence of no return.

---

10 I have discussed this in 'Inscription: Of Truth to Size' in *Outside in the Teaching Machine* (New York: Routledge, 2009), pp. 201–16.

11 Khaled Ziadeh, *Neighborhood and Boulevard: Reading through the Modern Arab City* (Samah Selim trans., Hosam Aboul-Ela intro.) (New York: Palgrave, 2011). I use this phrase with the French nationalist irony reflected in François Cusset, *French Theory: Foucault, Derrida, Deleuze et Cie et les mutations de la vie intellectuelle aux États-Unis* (Paris: Découverte, 2003), translated as *French Theory: How Foucault, Derrida, Deleuze, & Co. Transformed the Intellectual Life of the United States* (Jeff Fort trans.) (Minneapolis: University of Minnesota Press, 2008).

Our series is young. I have described our goal with appropriate modesty: to translate theoretical material operating outside the Euro–US, not readily available to metropolitan readership but continuous with the episteme, even as 'hybridity' keeps the local elsewhere. Yet there are also singular enclaves in many places where teaching and thinking apparently take place in less continuous epistemic formation. To acquire texts from these enclaves would require the kind of preparation, partly traditionalist, partly anthropologistic, that I do not possess. Perhaps, if our initial forays succeed, we will be able to fling our net wider: particularly important in the context of sub-Saharan Africa, where strong theoretical writing in the imperial languages (also languages of Africa, of course) flourishes and holds influence. For theoretical writing in the indigenous languages, not necessarily imitating the European model, contained within internal conflict, avoiding the anthropologist in the name of tradition will be on our agenda, I had written earlier. *Pelong ya ka* by Sophonia M. Mofokeng (1962), completed in English translation as *In My Heart* by Nhlanhla Maake, is such a text.

Towards A History of the National-Popular in Bolivia by René Zavaleta Mercado was our inaugural text. We also published a passionate interpretation of Zavaleta's socio-historical, politico-theoretical journey by Luis Tapia Mealla. Zavaleta/Mealla's work emphasized our series' attempt to do a layered analysis of 'motley' societies, where the feudal co-exists with the capitalist and the democratic/modern. The need for such work today, when democracy is being destroyed by identity-politics everywhere, is urgent.

My hope is that this thinking will be itself wrenched into the gendered 'motley' by thinkers in the near future, without excuse/accusation—and the critique of 'postmodernism' will be thickened.

I have mentioned Khaled Ziadeh above. In his book *Neighbourhoods and Boulevards: Reading through the Modern Arab City*, he describes the city of Tripoli in Lebanon. Ziadeh locates a non-Eurocentric modernity in the Ottoman café. And he describes how the French state 'Islamized' the city by building more than a hundred mosques.

Abdessalam Benabdelali, author of the book you are holding in your hand, himself a considerable translator, would not be 'Islamized'. This depends also in the difference between Morocco and Lebanon, between North Africa and West Asia, between Morocco–Algeria–Tunis and Lebanon–Jordan–Palestine–Israel. Egypt, Sudan, Ethiopia—'Africa' (or 'Lybia') to European antiquity stand somewhat apart from specifically 'French' theory. But for the rest, as we translate more Arab texts, we will make visible the diversity I have simply tabulated above.

Marouane Zakhir and Christian Hawkey's translation grasps the details of French postcoloniality astutely. I look forward to a text in the years to come that will foreground the pre-Islamic languages of a broad region not contained by the European borders of the modern 'Middle Eastern' nation-state, potentially bringing the book into the contemporary confrontation between nationalism and globalism. Can an elsewhere text supplement both?

We have just completed *Breaking the Chains*, by Dong Limin from China, a powerful critic of many accepted social gender paradigms. It should be available to you as you read this.

Our translators share with us the problems of translation for each unique text, at least hinting to the reader that, although the activity of translating is altogether pleasurable, to accept translations passively as a substitute for the 'original' closes doors. We will not give up the foolish hope that a careful translation, sharing problems, will lead to language-learning.

Read our series as a first step, then. Come to the projected conferences if they happen, where all of the authors and translators will gather, to ask: what is it to theorize elsewhere, in our world?

Gayatri Chakravorty Spivak

BOOK I

On Translation

Foreword

The Labyrinths of Translation

A student once asked me to recommend the best French translation of *The Arabian Nights*. He vaguely knew that the book had been translated many times into French, but he wanted to save effort and time by avoiding inaccurate or distorted translations. What does it mean to read different translations of one book? I answered that he should read the all translations in different languages, which surprised him. I told him that this is what I had done, as much as I could, when I was preparing my book *The Eye and The Needle*.

I benefited a lot from the many translations of the stories of 'Shahrazad', even from the unfaithful ones. I probably would not have finalized my study, or would not at least have finished it as it is, if it were not for insisting on the continuous comparison between the Arabic text and the attempts made to translate it, although my central concern was with the original text, or so it seemed.

Nevertheless, the benefits gained from these translations remained modest, slight and encompassed by a tinge of doubt. Who does not commend loyalty and fidelity to the text? Who does not vent their anger on cheating, deception and evasion? I used to see the work translators do as a denaturalization, an evident aberration, and at best an obtrusive and parasitic literary work.

Now that I have read Abdessalam Benabdelali's *Writings on Translation*, I view things differently. This is what usually happens with serious and innovative studies: they change our perspectives on things by posing new questions that reframe our postulations and what we used to believe in. Now, all translations of *The Arabian Nights*, even those which horribly change the text, appear to me precious and indispensable. They enrich the book and add to its connotations, meanings and images, some of which do not exist in the original version. We can imagine a final translation of the text (and who doesn't wish it?), but it will certainly be a sign of indifference and an indication of its decline and demise.

Abdessalam Benabdelali affirms that translation is 'a question of philosophy': it is its fundamental theme. In fact, each philosopher finds himself shifting back and forth between at least two languages even if he knows no other language except his mother tongue. Is it possible to imagine a book in philosophy, whatever its language, without foreign words? In this respect, it is not a coincidence that al-Jāḥiẓ talks about the *tarjumān* (the translator) in his work *Kitāb al-Ḥayawān* (The Book of Animals) while discussing Greek philosophy, nor is it a coincidence to find, nowadays, someone who reads French philosophy as a translation of German philosophy. One of the paradoxes that Abdessalam Benabdelali points out is that the German readers resort to the French translation of Hyppolite to understand Hegel's *Phenomenology of Spirit*.

The history of philosophy is essentially the history of translation. The latter can take on an explanatory and commentary aspect, as is the case with Ibn Rushd. To study Aristotle means to explain his texts, transform them from one language to another and from one discourse to another. It is this transformation which reinvigorates and animates philosophy. According to Derrida and Benabdelali, translation breathes life into texts and transfers them from one culture to another; the text lives only because it is at the same time translatable and untranslatable. The responsibility of the transformation of the text is not incumbent on the translator alone, but the language itself has a greater share of responsibility, for the language into which we translate the text has its particular rituals and requirements. The target language forces into the translated text issues that do not exist in its original version, thus the translator finds himself obliged to render what he doesn't want to render. Sometimes, the language refuses to cooperate with the translator and takes delight in his powerlessness and paralysis: Who can, for instance, translate into French the phrases *ammā baʿd* and *layta shiʿrī*?[1] Who can translate *ammā baʿd* into Arabic itself?

This is because translation exists even within the same language. 'Is there unity even within the same language?' asks Benabdelali. 'We all experience multilingualism within the same language', he answers. We read, for instance,

1 Translators' note: Literally translated into English as: 'but after' (*ammā baʿd*) and 'I wish my poetry' (*layta shiʿrī*).

The Arabian Nights in the Arabic edition of Bulāq, and we do not pay attention to the fact that this version is a clear 'translation' (transcription) of a text written in the vernacular.[2] We were obliged to wait for the edition of Muhsin Mahdi to be sure of this fact. The Arabic origin is not as clear as one may think—if we are permitted to speak at all about the 'origin' of *The Arabian Nights*, which is based on an illusion or a beautiful, passing wish.

Abdessalam Benabdelali's book is the first philosophical study of its kind on translation in contemporary Arab culture. Through translation, Benabdelali reappraises essential philosophical issues, such as identity and difference, origin and copy, unity and diversity, self and other. Sometimes, he resorts to allusion and insinuation, as when he remarks that 'the most flourishing eras of thought usually coincide with the prosperity of the translation movement.' This immediately leads the reader to think of the decline and atrophy of translation in our society and to contemplate with regret our cultural sphere, which no one could describe as prosperous. How many novels have we transferred into Arabic since Independence? The benchmark of translation is, unfortunately, never mistaken.

Among writers, there are those who make you feel from the first words that they address a particular group and talk in its name. This is not the case for Abdessalam Benabdelali, who addresses you in a voice that has a special tone and a unique imprint, and makes you feel as if he is addressing you personally and is writing for you. Within his calm and poised style, you feel a secret irony and a hidden, veiled suffering, the suffering of the philosopher who challenges ready-made ideas and tackles essential themes.

Abdelfattah Kilito

2 Translators' note: We used the term 'vernacular' to translate the word *dārija* used by the author because the latter may ambiguously refer to North African dialects.

Introduction

Translation Is a Philosophical Question

It is known that the question of translation has numerous facets. It was and is still addressed by writers and linguists as well as philosophers. However, the question of translation today is incontestably a question of philosophy, not in the sense that philosophy has to defer to it, but in the sense that translation today has become an issue of thought in its attempt to reread its heritage and surpass it. Besides, philosophy's main issue, since Plato, has been that of the model and its reproduction.

Therefore, when we say that translation is a question of philosophy, we mean, above all, that we can approach the question of philosophy through the issue of translation. Hence, the following pages should be understood as a means, among others, to undermine metaphysics and dismantle its structure.

Behind the story of translation, there is the myth of the Tower of Babel, which we find necessary to quote here as it is found in the Book of Genesis 11:1–9 (NRSV):

> Now the whole earth had one language and the same words. And as they migrated from the east, they came upon a plain in the land of Shinar and settled there. And they said to one another, 'Come, let us make bricks, and burn them thoroughly.' And they had brick for stone, and bitumen for mortar. Then they said, 'Come, let us build ourselves a city, and a tower with its top in the heavens, and let us make a name for ourselves; otherwise we shall be scattered abroad upon the face of the whole earth.' The Lord came down to see the city and the tower, which mortals had built. And the Lord said, 'Look, they are one people, and they have all one language; and this is only the beginning of what they will do; nothing that they propose to do will now be impossible for them. Come, let us go down, and confuse their language there, so that they will not understand one another's speech.' So the Lord scattered them abroad from there over

> the face of all the earth, and they left off building the city. Therefore it was called Babel, because there the Lord confused the language of all the earth; and from there the Lord scattered them abroad over the face of all the earth.

Thus were the sons of Adam prevented from imposing their language as the language and were condemned to multilingualism and translation.

Instead of construction, philosophy today seeks deconstruction. Instead of the construction of the tower—a unique language, a unique meaning and a unique identity—philosophy today presents deconstruction—a disassembly of the structure, perturbation [*al-balbala*], translation, difference and diversity . . . No wonder that the strategy of deconstruction aligns with that of translation—translation becomes a question of philosophy, and thought becomes a transformation and translation of metaphysics.

1
Translation and Metaphysics

Is translation possible? Metaphysics' answer from Plato to Hegel—passing by Leibniz—is in the affirmative. As long as meaning, which precedes writing and language, is the most important component in writing, it can be transferred from one language to another and from one sign to another. Translation as a transfer of semantic content, from one semantic form to another, is a possible task. It is true that translation poses some problems, since it seeks to produce a text that says 'the same thing' and has 'the same objective', nevertheless, it is possible, provided that the essence of the translated text is not betrayed. The task and value of the translator lies in his ability to overcome the difficulties posed by the diversity of languages and the heterogeneity of cultures in order to produce a text that duplicates the original. The translator's task is to bridge the gap that separates the text from its translation and the original from its copy, and to erase his own name in order to allow the writer of the original text to speak another language without losing his identity. The translator wants to write the text in the name of its author, to write it without putting his own signature on it. He wants to intervene without intervening and to appear to better disappear.

The possibility of apprehending the original text in its essence and then translating it and reproducing it is not a simple operation, but it constitutes the very structure of metaphysics—the Platonic structure of metaphysics. Platonism is not fundamentally about the distinction between the world of essence and that of appearance, the intelligible and the sensible, the idea and the image, the original and the copy—the model and the simulacrum. On the contrary, Platonism, as Deleuze wrote, is the examination of copies to reveal what belongs to the original and what does not:

> The distinction wavers between two sorts of images. Copies are secondary possessors. They are well-founded pretenders, guaranteed by resemblance; simulacra are like false pretenders, built upon a dissimilarity, implying an essential perversion or a deviation. It is in

> this sense that Plato divides in two the domain of images-idols: on one hand there are copies-icons, on the other there are simulacra-phantasms. We are now in a better position to define the totality of the Platonic motivation: it has to do with selecting among the pretenders, distinguishing good and bad copies or, rather, copies (always well-founded) and simulacra (always engulfed in dissimilarity). It is a question of assuring the triumph of the copies over simulacra, of repressing simulacra, keeping them completely submerged, preventing them from climbing to the surface, and 'insinuating themselves' everywhere.[1]

There is no need to assert that the unity of the original, its identity and congruence, is what establishes the status of the copy. Hence:

> Platonism thus founds the entire domain that philosophy will later recognize as its own: the domain of representation filled by copies–icons, and defined not by an extrinsic relation to an object, but by an intrinsic relation to the model or foundation. The Platonic model is the Same, in the sense that Plato says that Justice is nothing more than just, Courage nothing other than courageous, etc.—the abstract determination of the foundation as that which possesses in a primary way (en premier). The Platonic copy is the Similar: the pretender who possesses in a secondary way.[2]

The possible existence of iconic copies—copies which translate the original and transfer it—is what forms the structure of metaphysics as Platonism. It is true that Plato recognizes the simulacrum, but the simulacrum, for him, is the wicked and pretentious devil; it is the sophist who has nothing to do with philosophy or ideas, and who is unable to translate them, but who, despite that, misleads. The simulacrum is what complicates copying. It is what should be overcome to reach the world of meanings, to translate it and transfer it. That is the task of the philosopher.

---

1 Giles Deleuze, 'The Simulacrum and Ancient Philosophy' in *The Logic of Sense* (Constantin V. Boundas ed., Mark Lester and Charles Stivale trans) (New York: Columbia University Press, 1990), p. 256–57; 'Simulacre et philosophie antique' in *Logique du sens* (Paris: Minuit, 1969), pp. 295–96.

2 Deleuze, 'Simulacrum and Ancient Philosophy', p. 259; 'Simulacre et philosophie antique', pp. 298–99.

This task presupposes the existence of an ideal world, which is the world of originals, exactly as translation presupposes the existence of an original text—a text it seeks to copy, resemble and faithfully transfer: its iconic copy. Similar to Plato, who felt 'the difficulties of the philosopher', the translator should absolutely become aware of the difficulties he encounters. He often ends up saying that 'each translation is a betrayal'. This expression places us in an ethical atmosphere (where metaphysics situates the act of translation and the act of writing itself), where the text is perceived as an entity that requires us to respect it and treat it with 'intellectual honesty'.

The conception of metaphysics as translation is based on is based on essential propositions related to the concepts of writing, text, language, authorship and identity. Translation, in this way, presupposes that there is an original text that conveys and limits one meaning, and that this text is written for the sake of preserving, maintaining and communicating meaning, a meaning that the writer made in his text after deep meditation. It is a signed text that carries the name of the author, a text that has an identity that should not disappear in translation, a text that belongs to a mother tongue from which it obtains its characteristics. We should stop for a moment at these hypotheses, not to refute them in the name of counter-hypotheses, but only to question them.

Metaphysics wants to overcome the diversity of languages and to bring languages together. But is there unity even within the same language? What can be said if each linguistic system involves diversity? We all live multilingualism within one language, or at least deal with the dichotomy between the language of the father and the law, the language of the other, the language of the mother and the body. Can translation unify this diversity? What can be said about the numerous contemporary texts written in many languages, that borrow many words, or even quote various texts from different languages? There are always other texts belonging to the same language of the original that are closely related to it without necessarily being present in it. This is what Maurice Blanchot calls 'the proper translation of the original text'. Any text, explicitly or implicitly, involves different texts. In this sense, any text, though not translated, is a translation; the latter is not a secondary task that comes after the writing of the text.

These hypotheses postulate that we can overcome language and control it. However, does language so easily offer itself to us, as metaphysics pretends? Is it not true that language is the one that uses us to think? Is it not the one that speaks? The man, according to Heidegger, speaks only in his response to language when he listens to what it says:

> In its essence, language is not the utterance of an organism; nor is it the expression of a living thing. Nor can it ever be thought in an essentially correct way in terms of its symbolic character, perhaps not even in terms of the character of signification. Language is the clearing-concealing advent of Being itself. Language is the house of being.[3]

Additionally, is it not true that language conceals a sort of hegemony? In his distinction between 'language' and 'speech', Roland Barthes says that 'language is legislation, speech is its code.'[4] It is a classification that contains a sort of overpowerment. 'But language—the performance of a language system—is neither reactionary nor progressive; it is quite simply fascist.'[5] In this case, can't writing be against language? Or as Barthes also says, isn't writing a 'betrayal of language?'[6] Is writing not a deception and a betrayal? Does it not introduce strangeness into what language has made familiar? Is it not a displacement of language in language? If this is the case, language ceases to be an expression or a means of communicating meaning; rather it becomes a signifying practice within the context of social interactions and practices. As a result, the text will cease to be a conveyor of truth—*the* truth—but it will not cease to be the point of conflict around this truth. It will instead become the centre of conflicts between wills to power and the point of

---

3 Martin Heidegger, 'Letter on "Humanism"' (1946) (Frank A. Capuzzi trans.) in *Pathmarks* (William McNeil ed.) (Cambridge: Cambridge University Press, 1998), pp. 248–49; ' . . . L'homme habite en poète . . . ' in *Essais et conférences* (Paris: Gallimard, 1997), p. 228.

4 Roland Barthes, 'Lecture in Inauguration of the Chair of Literary Semiology, Collège de France, January 7, 1977' (Richard Howard trans.), October 8 (Spring 1979): 3–16; here, p. 5. Roland Barthes, *Leçon* (Paris: Éditions du Seuil, 1978), p. 12.

5 Barthes, 'Lecture', p. 5; *Leçon*, p. 14.

6 Barthes, *Leçon*, p. 16.

encounter between differing perspectives. The text, in this case, will not be able to restrict meanings, but it will inevitably spill over. If the translated text itself is not a means of communication, if it is not a restriction of meaning, can translation, as a copy that conforms and transfers the original, be meaningful? Or will it become impossible?

It seems that the question about the possibility of translation is meaningless, since there is a translation and, rather, translations of the same text. To remain in the context of philosophy, it is sufficient to mention some of Aristotle's books, which were translated from Greek and other languages. We have second- and third-degree translations of many of his books. What is important is that all these translations do abrogate one another. On the contrary, some translated texts concern us today only because of their 'distortion' of what is considered to be an original text. There are some translations which gain their historical importance from their betrayal of the original text. There are also littérateurs who take interest in translation just to escape and leave the ordinary, to become alienated from their familiar language. They come to translation precisely because of the 'betrayal' and the strangeness it involves. In this respect, Blanchot draws our attention to the reason French classical literature stuck to old cultures and languages, in search of an alienation that sought to promote the ordinary language to the level of the translated language (an ancient language which is considered a noble one).

> To transpose a Greek or Latin work into French was enough to accomplish the essential part of a creative act. [. . .] In the preface to *Oedipus*, Corneille regrets having lost the advantage of being only a translator. The moderns assuredly go further. *Translated from Silence*, that work by Joe Bousquet, is like the wish of an entire literature that would like to remain a translation in its pure state, an unburdened translation of something to be translated, an effort to retain, of language the only distance that language seeks to keep with regards to itself and that must, if pushed, result in its disappearance.[7]

7 Maurice Blanchot, 'Translated From . . . ' in *The Work of Fire* (Charlotte Mandell trans.) (Stanford, CA: Stanford University Press, 1995), p. 177. Maurice Blanchot, 'Traduit de . . . ' in *La part du feu*, NEW EDN (Paris: Gallimard, 2001), p. 174.

In this sense, translation is promoted to the level of creative writing itself:

> [T]he translated text mimics the effort of creation from the ordinary language in which we live, acquire existence, and are immersed. Translation seeks to give life to another language that seems to be the same language, though constituting its absence and difference, a difference which is perpetually acquired and constantly hidden.[8]

Translation breathes life into texts and transfers them from one culture to another; the text lives only because it is simultaneously translatable and untranslatable. If it is possible to translate a text into a final translation, it dies, both as a text and as writing, because the faithful imitation 'tends to unmake the work of translation, insofar as it acclimates it and thus takes away from it the privilege of the ambiguity, of the instability that make so many great translated works extraordinary'[9]

If translation seeks to be final, to present a copy that conforms to the original and to make from the translated language a mirror which reflects the original text, then it would be using a specific kind of language, a state which should necessarily be transformed. The instrument of translation is a living language, and its mirror is condemned to be broken. 'While a poet's words endure in his own language, even the greatest translation is destined to become part of the growth of its own language and eventually to perish with its renewal.'[10] In this sense, the translator is a creator in another language, or, more precisely, a creator in language itself. Therefore, it is not necessary for the translator to transfer the text and copy it, or to communicate its original meaning, because translation 'is not communication or the imparting of information'.[11] The task of the translator, as we have said, is to permit the text to survive and become perpetual because 'For in its afterlife—which could not be called that if it were not a transformation and a renewal of

---

8 Blanchot, 'Translated From', p. 190 [translation modified]; Blanchot, 'Traduit de', pp. 186–87.

9 Blanchot, 'Translated From', p. 180; 'Traduit de', p. 177.

10 Walter Benjamin, 'The Task of the Translator' in *Selected Writings, Volume 1: 1913–1926* (Cambridge, MA: Harvard University Press, 1996), p. 256. Walter Benjamin, 'La tâche du traducteur' in *Œuvres*, VOL. 1 (Maurice de Gandillac, Rainer Rochlitz and Pierre Rusch trans) (Paris: Gallimard, 2000), p. 250.

11 Benjamin, 'Task of the Translator', p. 253; 'La tâche du traducteur', p. 245.

something living—the original undergoes a change',[12] that is, it develops and procreates because the translations of a text constitute its 'history', a history of conflict and difference. The goal of metaphysics is to reduce the linguistic, cultural and ideological difference to a unified entity. Most of the questions that arise about translation have the aim of overcoming difference; however, without this difference, the linguistic difference in the first place, translation would not be necessary or possible. For, according to Derrida, in the limits where it appears to be possible, 'in the limits to which it is possible, or at least appears possible, translation practices the difference between signified and signifier. But if this difference is never pure, no more so is translation.'[13] Therefore, instead of translation, Derrida suggests the notion of *transformation*, that is, 'a regulated transformation of one language by another, of one text by another'.[14]

Translation can only be a series of transformations; a transformation of both reading and writing. Unlike metaphysics, translation does not want to be a copy that conforms to the original, to match the original or to be the other itself. On the contrary, translation is a strategy for birthing differences and grafting the other into the self. It is what opens the text and opens the language to the exterior. Thanks to this transformation, many books acquire a value that surprises the literature they previously belonged to and take on certain characteristics which would not have been recognizable before. In this context, Blanchot states:

> French readers are surprised by the influence exerted by their realist writers (particularly Maupassant) over foreign writers who seem to us a bit unrealistic. Therefore, we get astonished when we know that Flaubert was the mentor of Kafka.[15]

---

12 Benjamin, 'Task of the Translator', p. 256; 'La tâche du traducteur', p. 249.

13 Jacques Derrida, 'Semiology and Grammatology' in *Positions* (Alan Bass trans.) (Chicago, IL: University of Chicago Press, 1982), p. 20. Jacques Derrida, 'Sémiologie et grammatologie' in *Positions* (Paris: Minuit, 1972), p. 31.

14 Derrida, 'Semiology and Grammatology', p. 20; 'Sémiologie et grammatologie', p. 31. In fact, we consider this concept of translation as a transformation of an introduction used by Heidegger to introduce the translation of the first part of his questions in 1932. See Martin Heidegger, *Questions I et II* (Paris: Gallimard, 1990), pp. 10–11.

15 Blanchot, 'Traduit de', p. 175.

Nevertheless, we should not understand transformation as unidirectional. Translation does not only transform the translated text, but, at the same time, it also transforms the translating language. The translator, as Benjamin says, breaks the decaying barriers of his language: Luther, Voss, Hölderlin and George have expanded the boundaries of the German language.[16] We can also mention what happened to French writing when it opened itself to American literature and began to translate it. It is sufficient to cite what Jean Paulhan said about Camus's *Stranger*: 'it is Kafka written by Hemingway.' Translation, therefore, is not only what guarantees the survival of the text, its development and proliferation, but also what guarantees the survival of language and thought. The essence of translation as transformation is present even within the same language. That's why Heidegger states, 'Therefore, the essence of translating does not consist in two different languages entering into a dialogue.'[17] It often happens that 'the same speech, whether pronounced or written in the mother tongue, needs an interpretation; hence, there is always translation by necessity even within the original language itself.'[18] Perhaps this is what justifies the existence of dictionaries, which do not transfer a language to another, but translate between the same language. What constitutes the essence of translation is not its shift between languages, but the fact that it is an interpretation, for 'interpretation and translation are, in the core of their essence, the same.'[19] It appears that the French term *traduction*, together with its Italian equivalent *traducere*, came into use in the beginning of the fourteenth century to replace the terms 'translation' and 'interpretation', and to restore the glory to the Greek term *hermenia*. Translation, according to Heidegger, is the mental operation through which we appear in front of *nous traduire* [we translate]—the other's thought and language—like a criminal appears in front of the court. He says, 'We shall try to translate Anaximander's saying. This requires that we bring hither into our German language what is said in the Greek. To this end it is necessary

16 Benjamin, 'Task of the Translator', p. 258.

17 Martin Heidegger, *Heraclitus* (Julia Goesser Assaiante and S. Montgomery Ewegen trans) (New York: Bloomsbury, 2018), p. 50. Martin Heidegger, *Heraklit*, Gesamtausgabe, VOL. 55 (Frankfurt am Main: Vittorio Klostermann, 1979), pp. 63–64. Quoted in *Cahier Heidegger* (Paris: L'Herne, 1983), p. 456.

18 Heidegger, *Heraklit*, pp. 63–64.

19 Heidegger, *Heraclitus*, p. 49; *Heraklit*, pp. 63–64.

that, before the translating, our thinking is translated into what is said in Greek,'[20] that is, before what Anaximander said and what he did not say; what he thought and what he forgot; what is thought and what is unthought. But this unthought, this forgotten—is it the spirit of the text that metaphysics talks about? Is it its hidden meaning, its original meaning and its truth? If it is not the case, then what is this forgotten that hides behind revelation? It is the nothing but disappearance itself, replied Heidegger.[21]

We have already said that the text, even if it does not conceal an original truth, is nonetheless the object of conflicts about truths. If there is no truth to betray, there is still a game of truth—a game of infinite betrayal. In translation, as in any writing, there is no effective possession of truth. There is nothing but phantasm, passion and desire to possess truth without the existence of a true meaning. There is nothing to betray and no one to betray in the text, but betrayal is a characteristic of writing itself.

This means that translation, like any writing, cannot but be subsumed under the field of conflict of desires and the will to power or even the will to will. This will invaded the domain of translation itself in what is called 'technical translation'. This type of translation does not deviate from metaphysics. It is rather, like the technique, 'the perfection of metaphysics'.[22]

Technology, states Heidegger, is a form of reality and a way by which being reveals and unveils itself. It is the way in which being disappears to better appear as a 'standing-reserve'. 'Because it is the supreme form of rational consciousness, [technology] goes hand in hand with the absence of meditation as organized inability to access a relationship with what merits questioning.'[23] Besides, technology threatens to reduce any revelation into a mere efficiency and effect, condemning the human being to wandering and distraction:

---

20 Martin Heidegger, 'Anaximander's Saying' in *Off the Beaten Track* (Julian Young and Kenneth Haynes eds and trans) (Cambridge: Cambridge University Press, 2002), p. 248. Martin Heidegger, 'La parole d'Anaximandre' in *Chemins qui ne mènent nulle part* (Paris: Gallimard, 1986), p. 396.

21 Martin Heidegger, 'De l'essence de la vérité' in *Questions I et II*, p. 182.

22 Martin Heidegger, 'Dépassement de la métaphysique' *in Essais et conférences* (Paris: Gallimard, 1997), p. 92: 'Nous prenons ici,' writes Heidegger, '"la technique" en un sens si essentiel qu'il équivaut à celui de la "métaphysique achevée"'.

23 Heidegger, 'Dépassement de la métaphysique', p. 100.

> Since real reality consists in the uniformity calculations carried by blue prints, man himself is cornered in this monotony and uniformity . . . The being expands in the absence of differentiation; that absence that cannot be guaranteed or controlled except in through efficiency and organization, which responds to the principle of productivity. The latter seems to lead to a hierarchical order, but in reality it is based on the absence of any hierarchy, for the purpose of production is monolithizing vacuity. It is clearly obvious that the absence of difference is what emanates from this principle.[24]

This absence is what 'technical translation' aims to achieve when it wants to subdue language to the principle of productivity, transforming it to codes and signs, unifying languages to produce one language.

We should, therefore, go beyond translation as metaphysics and technique and try to translate and transform metaphysics by releasing it from its anthological and ethical atmosphere. This surpassing is what was termed 'the reversal of Platonism', which is not the replacement of the world of meanings with the world of sensibilities, as Heidegger thought,[25] but a triumph of simulacrum copies over the iconic copies. Transformational translation is the one that glorifies simulacrum copies, but this does not mean that we produce just any copy and in any manner, for the 'simulacrum' is not an arbitrary copy. It is true that it wants to be a scandal for the law that freezes language and precipitates writing into the abyss of repetitions and ruminations. But, as such, the copy is not a simple deviation and distortion of a certain original, for copying (*nasakha*) is not metamorphosing (*masakha*) in Arabic. The simulacrum, according to Deleuze, is not a distorted copy; rather it 'harbours a positive power which denies the original and the copy, the model and the reproduction.'[26] Therefore, let's say that the simulacrum is a *nuskha* (copy), in the full and paradoxical meaning of this Arabic term.

---

24 Heidegger, 'Dépassement de la métaphysique', pp. 112–13. We also read in the book of *Paths That Lead to Nowhere*: 'The technique wants to organize the world. Whereas, this manner of organization is what regulates the harmony and the unity of production between all levels, i.e. degrees'. See Martin Heidegger, 'Pourquoi des poètes?' in *Chemins qui ne mènent nulle part*, p. 354.

25 Heidegger, 'Dépassement de la métaphysique', p. 91.

26 Deleuze, 'Simulacrum and Ancient Philosophy', p. 261; 'Simulacre et philosophie antique', p. 302.

Nasakha is one of the terms that constitute a scandal to the logic of metaphysics, which is the logic of limitation and identity. It is one of the terms that conceal contradictory meanings, which are both difficult to limit and hard to translate. It is one of the terms that we can't translate even within Arabic. In its attempt to define *annaskh*, the dictionary *Lisān al-ʿArab* states: '*annaskh* is the abrogation of something and its replacement by another. It is the substitution of a thing by another which is different. It is also transferring something, as it is, from one place to another.'[27]

There is *nasakha* in the sense of annulling, abrogating and removing, and *nasakha* in the sense of transferring. Translation is abrogation, continuity and cancellation. It is a transfer and a transformation of meanings, but it is not a transfer of an original meaning, for the meaning exists only in its return, in its repetition, 'And there is no repetition possible without the graphics of supplementarity, which supplies, for the lack of a full unity, another unit that comes to relieve it, being enough the same and enough other so that it can replace by addition.'[28] Fidelity in translation, as Benjamin writes, is 'the significance of fidelity as ensured by literalness is that the work reflects the great longing for linguistic complementation. A real translation is transparent; it does not cover the original, does not block its light.'[29]

The translating copy permits the text to procreate from one language to another, as well as the procreation of the language itself. However, procreation, here, is not a mere transmigration of souls that does not affect the body of writing.

Finally, is translation possible?

It is at the same time possible and impossible. This being the case, there are texts and there are languages.

---

27 Ibn Manzur, *Lisān al-ʿArab* (Dictionary) (Beirut: Dar Sadir, 1955–56).

28 Jacques Derrida, 'Plato's Pharmacy' in *Dissemination* (Barbara Johnson trans.) (London: Athlone, 1981), p. 168. Jacques Derrida, *La Dissémination* (Paris: Éditions du Seuil, 1972), pp. 194–95.

29 Benjamin, 'Task of the Translator', p. 260; 'La tâche du traducteur', p. 257.

2
Translation and Acculturation

The relationship between contmporary French philosophy and German thought offers us a good example that invites us to pause and reflect—not only to understand the act of translation, but perhaps also to realize its very essence. Anyone interested in the development of this relationship may conclude that French philosophy can be read as a translation of German thought, and that the history of that philosophy is nothing but a translation movement that has never been satisfied with itself. However, what elicits the observer's attention is not only the fact that great French philosophers are translators of German texts,[1] but also the fact that their translations abrogate one another. The phenomenon that characterizes the French translation movement is that of reconsideration. This does not merely apply to the German texts that were famous for their difficulties, such as those of Heidegger, but also for the texts of Freud, Nietzsche, Hegel, Husserl and Marx. It is known that new attempts are made today to retranslate the works of Freud under the leadership of Laplanche and Pontalis, Nietzsche by Gilles Deleuze, and Hegel by Labarrière, etc.

What can we deduce from this? Shall we say that the French language was incapable of translating Freud, Nietzsche and Hegel during the time of S. Jankélévitch, Henri Albert, Alexandre Vialatte and Jean Gibelin, and that it only became capable of doing so with the emergence of a new generation of translators? Or shall we say that those previous translations were sufficient and suitable for an era in which the great French philosophers paid no attention to these names? What is known, for instance, is that Sartre himself wasn't a reader of Nietzsche. He read only two books by Freud, according to Beauvoir, and he 'knew' only the 'early works' of Hegel. Shall we conclude that Nietzsche, Heidegger and even Hegel, the author of the *Science of Logic*,

---

1 This is true not only for the philosophers of the day, such as Althusser in his translation of Feuerbach, or Derrida in his translation of Husserl, and Foucault in his translation of Kant, but also for the philosophers of the past, such as Victor Delbos, Jean Hyppolite and Paul Ricœur . . .

were not able to speak French before, that they become able to do so only today, and that the current translations of their texts are definitive? Or shall we say that German thought started to survive in and through French, to the extent that German readers now consult Hyppolite's translations as a means to understand the original German text of the *Phenomenology* itself?

We can answer all these questions only if we question the derogatory meaning of the expression: 'French philosophy can be read as a translation of German thought.' The same saying reminds us of the expression that was and still applies to Islamic philosophy in its relationship to Greek thought. That meaning is nothing but an extension of the pejorative meaning and the secondary status attributed to the act of translation. For the same expression can be translated as: 'German thought only survives in French translations'. In this way, the task of translation is reversed and promoted. Translation, then, is what breathes life into texts and transfers them from one culture to another and from one language to another. Hence, it is true that Nietzsche (and Heidegger, and Freud) has no life today, except in the writings of Foucault, Derrida and Lacan. He lives only because he speaks French, exactly like Aristotle, who wouldn't have survived if he hadn't spoken Syriac, Arabic, Latin and German. Nietzsche will not survive or be resurrected unless he speaks another language. If and when he finds his final translation, he will die. And if it is possible to translate a text as a final translation, it will die as a text and as writing. The text lives only because it is both translatable and untranslatable. Even if a translation seeks to be final, to posit a copy in conformity with the original and to turn the translated language into a mirror that reflects the original text, it will nevertheless have used a historically specific form of the (target) language, a form that will necessarily change—indeed, it will have used a historically specific form of thought, which will inevitably be exchanged for another. Let us recall what Marx said about Jean Roué's French translation of *Capital*. For Marx, though the translation was not an 'equal copy' of the German text, it aligned with French thought at the time of its publication—implying that it would not have aligned with French thought had it appeared at a different time. This is precisely what today's translation of *Das Kapital* reflects, which even led to revisions of the translation approved by the author himself, and prompted the 'new' readings of the book to accompany new translations.

The destiny of great and perfect translations is disappearance. In a sense, the translator is a creator in another language or, more precisely, a creator in language. Therefore, it is not necessary for him to transfer the original text and copy it, nor to care for the communication of its original meaning, for 'its essential quality is not communication or the imparting of information.'[2] The task of the translator is to permit the transfer of the text from one culture to another, allowing it to remain alive and perpetual. There is no meaning in transfer without transition, no survival without transformation and renewal, and no renewal without development and proliferation.

Yet, we should not understand transformation here as unidirectional. Translation does not only transform the translated text, but also transforms the translated language. Here, we can evoke what happened to writing in French when it opened itself up to American literature. This is exactly what we witness in Arabic today, as we start to sense the traces of French, English and Spanish in its texts. Translation, therefore, is not only what guarantees the life, development and proliferation of the translated text, but also what guarantees the life, development and proliferation of language and thought. For this reason, perhaps, the most flourishing eras of thought usually coincide with the prosperity of the translation movement. In this sense, translation is not a sign of dependence, reproduction, stagnation and death, but rather a sign of openness, volatility, fertility and life.

This also applies within the same language, because the essence of translation as an act of transformation is present even within a single language itself. Heidegger wrote, 'the essence of translating does not consist in two different languages entering into a dialogue.' 'That is why, even in one's own language, translation is constant and necessary, given the fact that the words and texts of the mother tongue are often open to interpretation.'[3] Don't we feel while reading some traditional Arabic texts that we need to translate and transfer them into contemporary Arabic? Any language, as long as it is alive, inevitably proliferates, and its lexicon grows. For this reason, language lives in translation and by translation. In this sense, there is an auto-translation

---

2 Benjamin, 'Task of the Translator', p. 253; 'La tâche du traducteur', p. 245.

3 Heidegger, Heraclitus, pp. 49–50; *Heraklit*, pp. 63–64. Quoted in *Cahier Heidegger*, p. 456.

that corresponds to what we can call auto-acculturation, for acculturation not only confronts one culture with another, but also alienates a culture from itself.

Acculturation is what introduces the other to the self, and makes a culture confront and oppose itself. It is what makes a language need an interpretation and a translation in order to express itself and stay abreast of acculturation. Whether this happens within one culture or various cultures, translation remains the instrument of acculturation.

3
In Praise of Betrayal

Numerous expressions link translation to notions of fidelity and betrayal. The most famous are: 'any translation is an act of betrayal' and 'an ugly and faithful translation is better than a beautiful and unfaithful one'. In what follows, we will try to examine the philosophical and poetic premises which justify this linkage, for it is based on a well-defined philosophy of identity and difference and on a definite theory of text and writing. How can the translator arrive at this linkage?

By first taking for granted the fact that meaning, which pre-exists both writing and language, is the most important element in writing, this meaning can be transferred from one language to another, from one sign to another. Hence, translation becomes a transfer of semantic content from one form of content to another. This is a possible and legitimate operation. It is true that translation poses some difficulties, since it aims to produce a text that says the same thing and has the same objective, but it remains a possible process. The task and value of the translator are manifest in his ability to overcome the difficulties posed by the diversity of languages and the heterogeneity of cultures. His task is to overcome cultural and linguistic differences, and to erase his name in order to allow the writer of the original text to speak in another language without losing his identity.

Translation, in this conception, presupposes that there is an original text that conveys and defines one meaning, and that the text is written to preserve, maintain and communicate this meaning, a meaning which the writer makes in his text after a deep meditation. It is a signed text that carries the name of the author; a text that has an identity which should not be lost in translation. A text that possesses sanctity and demands to be treated with 'intellectual honesty'. Therefore, the translator feels that he has an ethical responsibility, that he is indebted, that he is entrusted with something: he has a duty to write the text in the name of its author—but to write it without writing it, to intervene without intervening and to appear only to disappear.

This lofty goal inevitably leads the translator to feel many difficulties. When he realizes these difficulties, the translator decides that 'any translation is an act of betrayal' and regretfully asserts that 'an ugly and faithful translation is better than a beautiful and unfaithful one'. This attitude, then, presupposes a certain theory of the text and a definite conception of writing and language, based on a certain philosophy of identity and difference and on a theory of the model and its reproduction. We are not able, and it is not in our intention, to confront these beliefs and these theories with counter-beliefs and theories. Rather, we will be satisfied with raising some questions about them.

This attitude claims to bring languages together and to overcome their diversity so as to establish compatibility and unity. But is there unity even within the same language? What can be said if each linguistic system contains a certain degree of diversity? We all survive multilingualism within the same language. What, then, can be said about texts—and how many there are today!—that are written in multiple languages? Any text, explicitly or implicitly, involves other texts. Any text contains quotations and elements from other languages. A text can also use words that are foreign from the language in which it is written. In this sense, any text, even if it is untranslated, is a translation. Translation is not a secondary task that comes after writing the original text. So, in this sense, the translator is an author, and the author is a translator.[1] The translator is not that undesirable guest who is left outside and barely gets access to the book, whose name is written in faded letters on the cover, and whose rights are rarely acknowledged—unlike the rights of the author.

And isn't this betrayal—'a deviation from the right path'—considered by modern poetic theory as the essence of writing? Is writing, as Barthes says, not 'a betrayal of language'? Is it not an evasion, a deception and a peculiarity introduced to our familiar sense of language? Is writing not a displacement of language and a destruction of its idols?

Furthermore, expressions such as those above start from the assumption that the term restricts, limits and determines the meaning, and that the text signifies one thing and has one interpretation. But what can be said if we adopt the contemporary semiological theory that considers the term to be both denotative and connotative, and that the text, once it is written, enters

1 Perhaps this is what the expression 'translation is a long quotation' means.

a spiral of infinite interpretations? Does translation then, as a copy that conforms to, transfers and reproduces the original, have any meaning? Which original copy will translation depend on? It must choose, from the copies of the original, one copy to translate. Then translation becomes a copy of a copy, an interpretation of an interpretation—that is, an interpretation in the second degree. This ethical view of the operation of translation, relating it to fidelity and betrayal, supposes that behind the act of translation there is an ethical person who has rights and duties—a person who is responsible for the translation. This view supposes that the one who translates is a person. But in fact, who translates? Or more accurately: What is that agent that translates?

Perhaps translation is related to an agent that transcends ethical individuals and persons, for the subject of translation is language itself. Accordingly, all ethics of translation collapse. The agent responsible for the act of translation is the translating language.[2] This, of course, does not mean that we deny the contribution—rather, the creativity—of the translator. However, this responsibility remains small in comparison to the responsibility and effectiveness of the translating language. All critical questions that might be raised about a translated text will remain, in our view, partial questions if they judge the translator to be the source of power or weakness, success or failure, betrayal or fidelity, without taking into consideration the reality of the translating language and the limits of the thought that thinks by means of this language in a specific time. Some Arabic translations that have appeared recently represent strong evidence for this idea. Some of our translators made great efforts to translate texts by Foucault and Lévi-Strauss. They took pains to advance Arabic—which does not yet assimilate the philosophical fundamentals of contemporary thought—to the level of these texts. However, their translations hardly drew any attention. They even remained absent from the Arabic cultural sphere. Probably the reason for this phenomenon is not so much the inability or incompetence of the translators as it is the existence

---

2 Perhaps language is the doer behind the act of thinking itself. According to Heidegger, language is the one that thinks. In the same context, Maurice Blanchot says: 'We conclude from the previous observations about language essential points. The most remarkable one is the impersonal characteristic of language, its independent and absolute existence, which Mallarmé talked about. This language does not suppose any person to speak it or to listen to it; rather it speaks to itself and writes itself.' Maurice Blanchot, *La part du feu* (Paris: Gallimard, 1972), p. 48.

of a factor that transcends individual abilities. This factor refers to the translating language itself, the thought that thinks by means of that language today, and the philosophical concepts that the language has been able—or has not yet been able—to assimilate.

If we admit that language is a living being, a historical being who translates, then the text itself will inevitably undergo various translations within the same language. Yet what is remarkable is the existence of different translations of the same text within the same language and at the same period of time.[3] This phenomenon is noticeable in the Arab world today, as if translation does not seek, in the first place, to present the translated text to Arab readers, but rather aims to domesticate the translating language, train it and familiarize it with the language of modernity. The act of translation, in this sense, is similar to the act of solving a mathematical problem, for the mathematician does not aim to know the result, but rather to follow the reasoning that leads to the same result through different methods. Even if he is provided with the solution, it is still necessary for him to discover, by himself, the process or processes of justification, if possible.[4]

There is no, and there will be no, single translation of the same text. Anyone who wants to translate texts is aware of this reality. He knows beforehand that this translation is not, and will never be, a copy conformed to the original—that is, 'the same of the other'. For if translation seeks to be final, claiming that it creates a copy conforming to the original and turns the translating language into a mirror that reflects the original text, then it must be using a specific instance of language and a specific instance of thought—an instance which will inevitably change. The instrument of translation is a living language, and its mirror is condemned to be broken. Besides, the destiny of the greatest translations is to die when the language of translation grows and is renewed. The translator, therefore, is a creator in another language—or, more accurately, a creator in language itself. For this reason, he should neither merely transfer and copy the text, nor translate it as a definitive

3 For instance, in Morocco there are three translations of Foucault's text *The Order of Discourse* and three translations of Roland Barthes's text *Elements of Semiology*. There are many examples of this, but what should be pointed out is the fact that all these translations have no relation to one another and do not reproduce one another.

4 Perhaps, for this reason, translation cannot do without the original text.

version. The text that ceases to be the object of translation does not reach this state because it has received its definitive translation in all languages, but because it is dead as a text and as writing. Translation is what breathes life into texts and transfers them from one culture to another. And the text lives only because it is both translatable and untranslatable. In this sense, betrayal and unfaithfulness are essential in every translation. Fidelity, as Benjamin says, is 'that the work reflects the great longing for linguistic complementation. A real translation is transparent; it does not cover the original, does not block its light, but allows the pure language, as though reinforced by its own medium, to shine upon the original all the more fully.'[5]

Perhaps this is what explains the emergence of certain texts in bilingual editions. They are mirror books, which, from the start, place before their readers the text and its original—the original and its copy—in a face-to-face way, recognizing the transparency of the copy and its essential and permanent reference to the original text. These publications ask the reader to intervene in order to examine the translation and produce a third text through the link and the marriage of the original text and the copy.

We have already said that translation cannot be a copy of the original, but rather a copy of a copy, because the original text has many interpretations and involves an excess of meaning. We can now say the same thing, but for a different reason: many books are not translated from their original languages, as we often have their translations of the second or third degree. What is important in these translations is that they do not exclude one another. There are many examples of this type of translation in contemporary Arabic thought. The majority of the translations that fed this thought are translations of translations. We can cite, for instance, the Arabic translations of the works of Freud, Nietzsche and even Hegel, as well as some great literary works of Dostoevsky that fed, and are still feeding, our intellectual formation. It is true that some people do not recognize these translations, but no one can deny the role they played in the Arab reader's representations and interpretations of these intellectuals and their books. No one, for example, can deny that the Arab reader knows Freud only through the Arabic translations based on his French translations, and that he knows only the French Freud.

5 Benjamin, 'Task of the Translator', p. 260; 'La tâche du traducteur', p. 257.

We all know that this Freud has a special history—this Freud by whom Sartre read only two books, according to Simone de Beauvoir; this Freud who was translated into French and is still being translated and retranslated.[6] No one, then, can deny the role that these 'treasonous' translations played.

There are, therefore, some translations which acquire their historical importance from their betrayal of the original text. Also, there are among the translated texts those that concern us today only because of their distortion of what was considered to be original.

In light of what has been said, it seems that we can now recover all those expressions which link translation with betrayal—but this time, not with a sense of regret or sorrow, but rather as a recognition that translation as a whole, like any writing, is an activity, a transformation and a reproduction (*iʿādat intāj*). Translating a text means transforming and reproducing it. The text will die, will be abrogated, only if it is no longer in a position to produce—only if it no longer raises any questions. In this case, it not only ceases to be an object of translation, but also ceases to be used to think and to be thought about; it does not circulate, is not interpreted and is not read—it ceases to be a text.

Translation is a reproduction, an abrogation and a continuation. It is a transfer and a transformation of texts. It is a transfer of two languages: the translating language and the translated language. Perhaps this is what al-Jāḥiẓ meant when he wrote:

> Once the translator (*tarjumān*) speaks two languages, we should know that he treats them with prejudice, because each of the two languages draws the other towards itself, borrows from it and opposes it.[7]

6 This, of course, does not mean that we do not have some important translations for Freud's books. It is sufficient to remember the Arabic translation of *The Interpretation of Dreams*, realized by Dr Mustapha Safouan; this translation is said to exceed the French translation of the same book. There is also the translation of Mannheim's book *The Ideology and The Utopia* by AbdelJalil Taher. This translation differs a lot from the French translation performed by Pierre Rivière, who eliminates a whole section from the book.

7 Al-Jāḥiẓ, *Kitāb al-Ḥayawān* (The Book of Animals) (Abdessalam Haroun ed.), VOL. 1 (Beirut: 1969), p. 76.

The translating language betrays not only the translated language, but also itself. Without this double betrayal, there would be no translation, and there would be no writing.

4
The Double Betrayal

I want to raise a question that appears, for some people, to be resolved—or at least to be a temporary issue. This question is linked with a phenomenon that we have begun to observe frequently in the contemporary Arab cultural sphere: the appearance of many translations that do not translate the text from its original language, but rather translate its translations and reproduce its copies. According to the Platonic schema, they are translations that do not produce the icon, but generate the simulacra. We have many examples of these translations not only in the domain of philosophy, but also in other domains such as literature and linguistics. To remain in the domain of philosophy, perhaps it is not an exaggeration to say that the majority of Arabic translations we have—and they are not many—of Kant, Hegel, Freud, Nietzsche, Marx or Heidegger were translated from languages other than the original.

The first direct question that should be raised here is: What is the value of these translations? Shall we consider them a double reproduction (*naskh*) and perversion (*maskh*) of the original texts—a double betrayal? Or shall we recognize in them, at least, a momentary value, while waiting for the appearance of 'real translations' that birth the original directly and not its progeny and offspring? Or shall we say, on the other hand, that these translations, whether we like it or not, participated in the education of many generations and helped us to learn about Hegel, Freud and Marx?

Even if 'real' and desired translations appear, they will not make us dispense with these 'perverted' translations that played the role of the text—and this is so not despite their distortion of meanings, but maybe by virtue of this very deviation.

Now, we realize that this question is not as easy as it may first appear. What concerns us here is not the search for a pleasing answer to our primary question, nor the judgment of these translations, but rather the attempt to raise some questions about translation through this phenomenon, which embodies the issue of translation in its most pathological state. The treatment of this question may lead us to rethink our conception of translation itself—and probably our understanding of the life of texts and the procreation of their meaning.

It is needless to prove, at the outset, that this 'phenomenon' does not concern Arab culture alone, nor does it concern Arab-Islamic culture only in the present. For Arabic, since its openness to other cultures—particularly Greek thought, which it did not encounter in its own language—engaged with that thought when it no longer lived in its original language. Rather, it lived in other languages. I will draw on this matter in my attempt to answer the previous questions, namely: that the text lives in one language but dies in another, and—more importantly—that the text, very often, does not remain alive in the language where it first appeared, the language in which and by which it was born, but instead lives on in another language—or rather, in other languages. The text, as Benjamin states, continues to live by virtue of translation.[1] The most famous example in philosophy is that of Aristotle, who spoke Greek and then stopped speaking it to speak Arabic, Latin and German—and maybe he is speaking in English today.

It is known that early Arabic translations of Greek thought were from Syriac, and not Greek itself.[2] Whatever our position on this matter, we cannot deny that these translations of the second degree had historical significance. They are the ones that fed Arabic Islamic thought in its beginnings, and through them, this thought came to know Greek wisdom. Or let us say that it would not have known Greek thought without the language in which it was alive—and that language was Syriac. Arabic would later play the same role when it, not Greek, transferred to the Latin world at the beginning of the European Renaissance the Greek thought that had already been translated, interpreted and reproduced.

It seems that these 'granddaughter translations' have their value and weight, even though we underestimate and even despise them. We find these feelings echoed by their translators as well, when they try in their introductions to apologize for their reliance on a language other than the original in which

1 Benjamin, 'La tâche du traducteur', p. 247.

2 See Abderrahmane Badawi, *La transmission de la philosophie grecque au monde arabe* (Paris: Vrin, 1968).

the text was written. They reiterate that they resorted to other translations of the text, and that they resorted to deception to get as close as possible to the original—such as when the translator, for instance, says that although he was unable to translate the text from the original German, he used the French translation and received assistance from the English and Spanish translations of the same text. We find that even the translator undervalues and feels dissatisfied with these translations of the second or third degree.

This position presumes that if any translation is in principle a betrayal, the translation of a text from a language other than its original is a double betrayal. The transition from the text to its translations, according to this position, is both a defeat and a blunder. It is a transition from the origin to its copies, from a model to icons, and from the world of idealism to the world of sensibilities. It is an operation of loss and impoverishment through which meaning diminishes gradually. The closer we get to the original, the closer we come to the light of real meaning, and the less we betray the translated text. Conversely, the further we move away from the original, the more the meaning gets lost and the betrayal is multiplied. In brief, we are dealing with a Platonic conception of reproduction.

But does this view not comprise a misunderstanding of the act of translation itself—or rather of the essence of translation, which above all is transformative in its essence, as we have seen? To answer this question, maybe it is necessary to start from two concerns:

First: what we used to call 'an original text' may itself conceal a translation or translations, in such a way that the first text, the starting text, becomes a second text; the original encompasses copies from other originals, and the model becomes an element that does not transcend icons, but resides side by side with them. Second: the existence of translations that are promoted to the level of 'the original text' itself.

Let us detail the second principle before the first, and start with a famous problem in the domain of philosophy. This issue is related to the translation of Hegel's book *Phenomenology of Spirit*, whose first part is translated into Arabic by Mustapha Safouane. The book's complete French translation, produced by Jean Hyppolite, did not appear until a century and a half after the publication of the German version. It is said that German readers, from the moment Jean Hyppolite's French translation appeared, began to resort to it as a way to understand the original text. I do not want to conclude from this that the French translation conforms to the original, or that it is a complete translation with no degree of betrayal. Rather, I can take the opposite direction and say that it is treasonous and transformative enough that it managed to bring Hegel's language closer to German readers.

Let us, then, go back to the translation realized by Safouane. We know very well that he translated from German, to the extent that his translation of Freud's book *The Interpretation of Dreams* exceeded the accuracy of the only known French translation. However, while Safouane translated the first part of the *Phenomenology* (using the original title that Hegel was to give it: *The Science of the Experience of Conscience*), I cannot imagine that he was able, whatever his degree of proficiency in German, to do it without the translation of Hyppolite—or, let us say, the text of Hyppolite that is no longer a French copy of Hegel's text, but rather its twin. We have a case before us now in which the reference to the copy is as necessary as the reference to the original.

I do not mean that this translation by Hyppolite is a definitive translation of the book. The main evidence for this is the appearance of two other French translations of the same book at the beginning of the 1990s. The first translation was completed by Jean-Pierre Lefebvre in 1991, and the second was conducted by Gwendoline Jarczyk and Pierre-Jean Labarrière in 1993.

We can also confirm that Hegel's text, since it is still alive in French, will see other translations—because translation, as we have already said, is what constitutes the life and history of the text. The translations of the text do not cease because it finally finds its perfect translation, but because it is no longer a matter of thought and ceases to live in other languages. What is important is that the appearance of the text's various translations in the same language does not mean that these translations are weak. Rather, it reflects the vitality of the text in that language. Perhaps this is what accounts for the fact that the 'new waves of reading' of Marx, Freud and Nietzsche were accompanied by waves of new translations of their books. Yet this does not mean in any way that some of these translations cancel out or eliminate each other. This is what happened—and will happen—to the translation of Hyppolite. Reaching the level of the original text, this translation that made Hegel familiar to German readers will undoubtedly be re-edited alongside the translations of *Phenomenology of Spirit* that came after it. In this context, we have a famous example in the domain of philosophy. It is Wittgenstein's *Tractatus*, one of the most important philosophical texts that appeared in German at the beginning of the twentieth century. It is known that French readers discovered this text through the translation made by Klossowski in 1961. This translation was used by the great specialists of Wittgenstein in France, such as Jacques Bouveresse. The year 1992 saw the appearance of a new translation of the *Tractatus* by Christian Delacampagne. What concerns us here is the commentary of Delacampagne on the two translations and his attempt to compare them. He takes as an example the last thesis, which is the most obscure of the theses presented in the book. Klossowski renders it as follows: 'Ce dont on ne peut parler, il faut le taire' (What we cannot talk about must be silenced), whereas Granger uses: 'Sur ce dont on ne peut parler, il faut garder le silence' (We must keep silence over that which we cannot talk about).

Delacampagne comments on the two versions of the same thesis: 'There is no doubt that Wittgenstein himself would find difficulty in resolving the question. Since the vigilant amateur is unable to do this in his place, he will surely find, in the comparison between their difference, a subject to reflect on.'[3]

It is as though the commentator wants to say that the true translation exists between the two translations: it is the game of their differences.

In light of this result, let us turn back to the first principle: that any text explicitly or implicitly conceals divergent texts which are translated from other languages. Any text involves texts and quotations from other languages. The text may also use terms foreign to the language of its writing, and even foreign expressions, such as *en Français dans le texte*. Let us, for instance, imagine that we want to translate a text by Habermas in which he discusses Derrida, who, in turn, converses with J. L. Austin. We will be faced with both an original text and copies all at the same time—face to face with a text written in German but quoting texts written in French, which, in turn, quote texts from English. Any text explicitly or implicitly involves divergent texts. This is what Blanchot calls a 'translation that is proper to the original.' In this sense, any text—even if it is not translated—is a translation, because translation is not a secondary act that comes after the writing of the original text. If we grant that the translator is an author, then we should also grant that the

3 *Le Monde* (17 December 1993).

author is a translator. And even in the cases where he finds the texts he wants to quote already translated, he modifies them and indicates it in the footnotes using expressions such as 'our modification' or 'the translation of so-and-so, with modifications'. This is what usually happens with Derrida, for example, in dealing with the texts of Hegel, Heidegger and Nietzsche. Any translation, though it starts from a so-called 'original text', is a translation of many translations and a copy of many copies. Contrary to the Platonic view, the reproduction of copies does not come after originals; it rather generates them. In this sense, Gilles Deleuze states: 'The simulacrum is not a degraded copy. It harbours a positive power which denies the original and the copy, the model and the reproduction.'[4] We are accustomed to posing the question of reproduction within a domestic ethical atmosphere that obliges the translator to respect the parents and the ancestors. Perhaps we should, on the contrary, imagine the relationship between the translator and the translated text as a relationship based on violence, and place it within a game of deceptions, cheating and evasion—the evasiveness of language that Barthes considers 'the essence' of writing and literature. If we start from this hypothesis, all those a priori categories that make us classify texts within scales, degrees and genealogical trees—which distinguish the parents from the progeny, and mothers from granddaughters—will collapse.

If we add to this the theory in contemporary poetics that the text, even if it is not translated, enters into an infinite spiral of interpretation immediately after its writing, then translation, as a copy that conforms to or starts from the original, becomes irrelevant. For which original can translation take as its reference? Every translation is a copy of another copy and an interpretation of another interpretation.

Whether we start from what we call an original text or from a translated text that speaks a language different from its own, we are never in front of an original and its derivations, a model and a copy, a text of the first degree and a text of the second degree. In fact, we are only in front of one of the moments of infinite reproduction. This is translation, and that is the generation of meanings.

4 Deleuze, 'Simulacrum and Ancient Philosophy', p. 262; 'Simulacre et philosophie antique', p. 302.

Anyone who seeks 'real' meaning will not find it in its purity in a separate world—better to look for it between texts and between translations, 'in the game of their differences'.

5
The Circle of Translation

In their attempt to illustrate translation and the work it does, some invite us to imagine a group of individuals sitting side by side in a circle. Each one of these individuals knows only the language of the two individuals sitting next to them. If the first enunciates an expression, the second will translate it to his neighbour, who, in turn, will transfer it to the next, and so on until the turn reaches its end.

They argue that the original expression will return to the starting point altered and distorted 'after the turn'. They also think that the wider the circle and the more languages and individuals, the more the expression is perverted and further from its original meaning.

In this brief discussion, we will try to question this image, hoping to take translation out of its circle. So, what does the image say?

It first (and foremost) says that translation is a betrayal of the original meaning; that the series of successive acts of betrayal leads to a dilution of meaning; that this dissolution occurs throughout the circle, and that this turning of meaning is a 'fall' where the meaning disappears in a decreasing function. This means the closer we come to the starting point—the source of meaning and the locus of the original—the closer we are to the light of the real meaning. Conversely, the further the distance, the more amplified the betrayal and loss.

The second idea which the image insists on is that the return to the starting point is necessary, and the confrontation of the final version with the original is obligatory. There is no way of avoiding this return, the tail of the circle to its head. This means that the act of generating meanings and transferring them through languages and texts is posed within a circular temporality based on the principle of eternal circularity. But, as we will see, this eternal circularity is not the return of the same (*le retour du même*); it is rather the return of the identical. In other words, this act of generating meaning is posed within a metaphysical concept of repetition which insists on the return to the starting point and the lost original.

Additionally, this transmission occurs orally and through individuals. The translator here is an ethical person, who, after all, is held responsible for the loss. The agents in this circular movement are individuals who are neither able to convey meanings faithfully nor to preserve them during the movement which brings them back to their origins and returns them to their families.

Before we move on to what we may consider counter-images to this image, we have to note that this logic cannot reach its furthest horizon. If we imagine the supposed model in its utmost form and assume a large number of individuals and languages—if we enlarge the circle as much as possible and agree with the logic of the collapse of meaning to its extreme limit—then we must conclude that the circle will not be completed, and that the meaning will continue diminishing and become utterly lost. This loss will have such a result that the translator before the last one will have nothing to transmit to his neighbour. If we stretch this logic to its furthest horizon, then it will collapse, as its circle will be cracked and its ring fragmented.

Does this mean that we have to place this operation in a linear trajectory, and say that reproduction does not occur through a procedure that brings down meaning from the world of models to the world of copies, but rather through a progressive process—throwing the translation into a linear temporality that makes meaning grow once it shifts from one language to another?

This is what Walter Benjamin perhaps means when he maintains that it is in its translations that 'the life of the original, in its constant renewal, experiences its latest and most extensive development',[1] that the task of translation is to allow the text to survive and that no translation would be possible if its ultimate essence was to resemble the original.

In contrast to the negative, moral and theological image, this one offered by Benjamin gives us a different idea about translation. It considers translation an operation that produces meaning, guarantees the life of texts and, from the start, allows for the difference of the copy from its original.

However, even though the translations of a text are what constitute its history, it is also a history that conceals conflicts and differences. What the first image—the theological image—presupposes is the reduction of linguistic

1 Benjamin, 'La tâche du traducteur', p. 249.

and cultural differences into a unity, and, even worse, the reduction of history and its imprisonment within a circle.

The first image is set up within the closure of the metaphysical circle, whereas this second image wants to be an open line towards the future and open-minded towards its opposite. Accordingly, this image sees that the existence of translation emanates from the existence of languages and cultures. Translation is nothing but an operation of infinite transformations and a perpetual reproduction of these languages and cultures.

This linear image presupposes that translation does not aim to be a copy conformed to the original and the other itself. It grants that translation is a strategy to reproduce the differences and introduce the other into the self. Translation is what opens language outward and opens up meaning to unexpected horizons.

This linear image, therefore, tries to surpass the circular image in all its diverse defects. It thrusts meanings into the effective movement of history and limits the hegemony and authority of the original. It strips translation of its moral aspect in order to consider it a transformation and reproduction.

However, it seems that this image is not content with its exaggerated optimism, but tends to push translation into a temporality that distinguishes chronologically between different modes of time, considering the future both a transcendence and an inclusion of the past. It thus neglects an essential issue in translation and in any act of reproduction (*istinsākh*), which is the perpetual return to the original text. In any translation, there is a continuous revision of the original text and its ceaseless repeated return.

In contrast to what this linear image of the translation movement suggests to us, translation does not occur from one copy to another that abrogates and surpasses its predecessor. Translation 'progresses' not by virtue of Hegelian transcendence, but by what Heidegger, after Nietzsche, calls 'the infinite return to origins' to confront them with their copies. The copy here does not exclude the original, but rather adheres to it, longs for it and evokes it in every moment. Here we are again before the notion of the eternal circular return and in front of the principle of repetition. Does this mean a return to a circular movement and to a theological concept of translation?

While presenting this circular image, we have already said that the theological concept of translation postulates treason because it assumes that there is an ethical person behind the act of translation. And we have already shown that translation is contingent on an agent who transcends moral persons, and that language itself is the translating self. Thus, all the ethics of translation, the metaphysics of translation and the theology of reproduction collapse. As a result, the circle implodes and fragments—not to be transformed, this time, into a straight line, but to produce circles that never cease to multiply.

6

In the Mirror of the Other

Is it possible to address the issues of translation and the question of the 'self', as opposed to the other apart from notions of fidelity and betrayal, and without relying on any conception of dialectics or a theory of alienation? To answer this double question, I suggest starting with an examination of two essential texts: The first is from the *Fragments* of Schlegel, while the other is from Abdallah Laroui's journal *Khawāṭir aṣ-ṣabāḥ* (Morning Thoughts). Schlegel says:

> The Arabs have highly polemical natures; they are the annihilators among nations. Their fondness for destroying or throwing away the originals when the translations are finished characterizes the spirit of their philosophy.[1]

In his journal, Abdallah Laroui writes:

> I received two letters from Beirut at the same time, each conveying the same request: permission for the translation of my book *L'Idéologie arabe contemporaine* into Arabic. What would have been the reaction of the Middle Eastern reader had I written the book in Arabic, as I had intended at the beginning? It would be indifference, undoubtedly. All communication that occurs between us—Moroccans, Arabs or Muslims—passes through the West, exactly as it is the case for Europeans with America today. In fact, this is the core of the book.[2]

1 Friedrich Schlegel, 'Athenaeum Fragments' in *Philosophical Fragments* (Peter Firchow trans.) (Minneapolis: MN: University of Minnesota Press, 1991), p. 49. Friedrich Schlegel, 'Fragment de L'Athenaeum' (229) in Philippe Lacoue-Labarthe/Jean-Luc Nancy, *L'Absolu littéraire* (Paris: Éditions du Seuil, 1978), p. 131.

2 Abdallah Laroui, *Khawāṭir aṣ-ṣabāḥ* (1967–1973) (Casablanca/Beirut: Arab Cultural Centre, 2001), pp. 71–72.

The issue that these two texts share and raise is related to the relationship between translation and the other. While the first text tries to define the relationship that classical Arabic culture established with the texts it translated into its language, the second tries to determine the relationship that contemporary Arabic culture holds with itself and its other, and the role that translation plays in this context.

Of course, we are not concerned here with the examination of the ideological content of Schlegel's text, nor do we need to test the degree of its literal truth. Let us simply ask whether the consequences that arise from its assertion reveal something about the reality of translation in our traditional culture.

To determine these consequences, let us first ask what Schlegel means by the destruction of the originals. He means that classical Arabic culture would adapt and domesticate any text it translated into its own language. It would subdue it and eliminate its foreignness, swallow it and integrate it within the circle of the self, considering it no longer other. Therefore, it quickly dispensed with the original after promoting it to the level of Arabic.

In the framework of this relation of power, in which all difference is suppressed, we understand that translation would be born complete from the first moment. We also understand that translation could only be unidirectional, moving from other languages into Arabic and not the opposite.

Classical culture considered Arabic the language of culture. The majority of knowledge carriers were non-Arab (*ʿajam*), and 'though some of them were Arabs in origin', as Ibn Khaldūn said, 'they were not native in language.' Nevertheless, Arabs used to feel that they were 'addressing only readers who master Arabic. The only form of translation they used to imagine is the transference into Arabic, or the explanation, commentary and glossary—that is, a translation within the same language.'[3]

The ancients' feeling of self-sufficiency, for they believed that their literature concerned only those who mastered Arabic, led them to impose an embargo on their culture. They were not only content to simply discard translation

3 Abdelfattah Kilito, *Lan tatakallam lughatī* [Thou Shall Not Speak My Language] (Beirut: Dar aṭṭali'a, 2002), p. 24.

from their thought, but 'worked, inadvertently, to make their books untranslatable' and created expressions that are difficult to translate.[4]

Perhaps this self-isolation is what explains the fact that our philosophers did not feel, at all, the need to establish the link between reinterpretation and explanation, and between retranslation and returning anew to the original text.

It is hard for us today to understand that a philosopher like Ibn Rushd, while he was reading (or rereading, to use a more modern phrase) Aristotle, did not feel the necessity to retranslate his book, similar to what we observe today with the greatest intellectuals. However, what is surprising is that this relationship still exists today among some of our intellectuals. Is this not the same relationship that we still have with the Greek texts? Who among us feels, while rereading *The Republic* of Plato or *The Organon* of Aristotle, the necessity to return to the originals of these texts? Rather, we notice the survival of this relation that excludes the other, even in modern texts.

It is sufficient to remember some texts such as Nietzsche's *Zarathustra* and Goethe's *Werther*, which were translated into Arabic a long time ago without having any impact, or attracting any attention, or raising a problem, or joining a new network of relations, or even entering into a dialogue with Arabic culture. In short, they are texts that were transferred into Arabic without being translated into it.

Before we return to wondering about the causes behind this phenomenon, let us try to determine the relation that links contemporary Arabic culture with its other through the text of Abdallah Laroui.

In contrast to the absorption of the other into the self, which marks classical Arabic culture, as we have seen, we find another form of absorption occurring in the opposite direction, which characterizes contemporary Arabic culture. Abdallah Laroui states that if he had written his book *L'Idéologie arabe contemporaine* in Arabic, its fate in the Arab world would have been neglect.

The most important idea confirmed by Laroui here is that the Arab reader is the one concerned with the text, even if it is written in a foreign language. Translation here becomes the means by which we reach the concerned reader. In order for the Arab reader to receive a text, it is preferable—

4 Kilito, *Lan tatakallam lughatī*, p. 24.

indeed necessary—for that text to reach him in the form of a translation. It must be transmitted to him through another language. In contrast to the first attitude, it is necessary here for the other to intervene as a mediator between the Arab author and the Arab reader, and between the Arab creator and the Arab critic.

To explain the Arabs' lack of interest in the same book, Laroui states on another page of his journal:

> When the book is critiqued by the French, many Arab critics will dare to do the same thing based on the opponent's responses. This behaviour confirms the argument of the book, which is that the Arabs always answer only questions posed by the West.[5]

It is as if the Arab intellectual today recognizes himself only through the other, and speaks his language only through another language. What we write and read acquires its meaning only in its translation. We write to translate, and we translate to write. Who among us can write today without translating? The majority of our texts are translations. Most of our writings are rewritings. Our originals are derivative texts. In such a context, how can we distinguish between genealogical origins and historical beginnings?

What is even stranger is when an Arab writer, after writing in a foreign language, resorts to translating this same work back into Arabic. This is exactly what happened to Laroui himself when he translated his book into Arabic. In his book *Lan tatakallam lughatī* (Thou Shall Not Speak My Language), Abdelfattah Kilito points out that some Arab novelists think of their potential translator while they are writing. They create according to the probable translation. 'They work hard to facilitate the task of the translator by avoiding the use of expressions and references that might not fit the style of another language.'[6] In most cases, they wait for the appearance of the translation of what they wrote, or they themselves facilitate the circumstances for their translation into many languages. It is only at this moment that they feel the value of their works.

We understand the meaning and significance of this when we know that a writer such as al-Jāḥiẓ, a poet such as al-Mutanabbī, or a philosopher like

5 Laroui, *Khawāṭir aṣ-ṣabāḥ*, p. 105.

6 Kilito, *Lan tatakallam lughatī*, p. 25.

Ibn Rushd never worked on the translation of their books into a language other than Arabic, and never hoped for, predicted or even imagined such translations. Our creative writing now happens in light of translation, as if the originals are effects of their translations. Even if it is necessary to talk about betrayal, we should say with Borges that 'the original is unfaithful to the translation'.[7]

We shouldn't ignore an important point stated twice in the previous excerpts from Laroui's journal. It is the idea in which Laroui asserts that the reality of translation in the Arab world confirms the content of *L'Idéologie arabe contemporaine*. The reality of translation is the reality of Arab thought and the reality of contemporary Arabic culture. This culture knows itself today only through the other, and more crucially, through the way the other perceives it. It does not experience translation as a flow of writing and publishing, but as a way of life and a mode of being.

In this way, we read and write our literature today only through a process of comparison, parallelism and 'translation'. Comparison concerns not only some specialists but anyone who seeks to discuss Arabic culture. The reader who examines an Arabic text immediately relates it, directly or indirectly, to a European text—or, more appropriately, he doesn't read it without relating it to a European text. In this way, he reads about Ḥayy ibn Yaqẓān only to compare him with Robinson Crusoe; al-Mutanabbī only to search for Nietzsche in him; *Risālat al-Ghufrān* (The Epistle of Forgiveness) only to discover *The Divine Comedy*; *al-luzūmiyyāt* (The Self-Imposed Compulsion) only to look for Schopenhauer; *Dalaʾil al-Iʿjāz* (Proofs of Inimitability in the Qur'ān) only to search for Saussure; *al-Munqidh min al-Dalāl* (Deliverance from Error) only to find Descartes; *Tahāfut al-falāsifa* (The Incoherence of the Philosophers) only to search for David Hume; and *Muqaddima* (Prolegomena) only through the eyes of Auguste Comte—'so woe to the authors who have no European correspondents'.[8]

However, this process of linking, as we know, goes even farther in its attempt to translate literary genres themselves. It raises questions about what corresponds to the 'novel', the 'play' and the 'essay' in Arabic literature. It also

---

7 Jorge Luis Borges, *Enquetes 1937–1952* (Paris: Gallimard, 1957), pp. 201–202.

8 Kilito, *Lan tatakallam lughatī*, p. 26.

poses questions as to what corresponds to *al-maqāma* outside Arabic literature.[9] It also seeks to know if *ʿilm al-ʿumrān* has a match in other cultures.[10]

Now that we have drawn conclusions from the two texts we used as a starting point for our reflection, let us inquire about what they have in common. Based on what we have seen, we can confirm that Arabic culture in both cases excludes difference, either by drawing the other towards the self or dissolving the self in the other, in such a way that the task of translation essentially consists of engendering nearness and eliminating strangeness.

Here, we are not trying to bemoan a lost identity, or to transform translation theory into a branch of some larger theory of alienation. We aim instead to pose the question of translation beyond fidelity and betrayal, away from any humanist tendency and without neglecting the reality of struggle, that is, the Babylonian state of all languages, the state of confusion and original misunderstanding that characterizes all readings, interpretations and translations. We aim to insert translation within the relations of power that determine being, characterize volition, control languages and dominate cultures. For the issue here is not a misfortune that afflicts one culture and avoids another.

In this way, it is necessary to return to an appositive clause quoted in Laroui's text, in which he compares the relationship of Arabic culture with Western culture to the relationship of Europeans with Americans. It is sufficient to remember that many French writers now approach French readers through English. The most important examples are Pierre Bourdieu and Jacques Derrida (who wrote his essential text about translation in English).[11]

---

9 Translators' note: *Al-maqāma* refers to a type of short, episodic narrative pioneered by Badīʿ al-Zamān al-Hamadhānī in the fourth century AH (tenth century CE). It centres on a clever but impoverished hero who recounts amusing adventures or exploits in a witty, satirical and critical style. The purpose of *al-maqāma* can be to advise, persuade, entertain or even beg.

10 Translators' note: *ʿilm al-ʿumrān* is a social science that studies human civilization, urbanization and ways of life. It examines how people shape their communities, settlements and built environments. Ibn Khaldūn is regarded as one of the founding figures of this field, laying its foundations in his seminal work the *Muqaddima* (Prolegomena).

11 Jacques Derrida, 'Des tours de Babel' (1980) in *Psyché: Inventions de l'autre* (Paris: Galilée, 1987), pp. 203–35.

It is inevitable that translation occurs between languages that are linked to each other by relations of power. Sometimes, these relations are exploited to enter into conflict with the foreign language so as to subdue it and eliminate all that is indomitable in its texts. Here, translation is not problematic; it is not defeated in front of the text, nor does it stop at 'the untranslatable' or at what bears witness to foreignness, remoteness, distance and altruism—that is, what refuses submission and obedience. Translation here is not a strategy to generate differences that open the language to *its* exterior and open the foreign—*qua* foreign—to the space of the translated language.

For this openness depends on the recognition of the other as another and on stopping at what is 'untranslatable', as Goethe confirms in one of his letters:

> [W]e must not get into an immediate conflict with the foreign language. We must reach the untranslatable and respect it; for therein lies the value and character of every language.[12]

Stopping at 'the untranslatable', of course, disagrees with the destruction of originals. On the contrary, it is an implicit recognition of the permanent need to refer to origins—to return to them and to frequent them. It is an affirmation that translation is a continuous creation, that it cannot be the other in itself, *le même de l'autre* ('the same of the other'), and that it is not the same text that the author would write if he were to speak the language of the translator. It is also an assurance that the distance between the self and the other cannot be completely excluded, that the translated text continues to be linked to its original, and that any translation remains transparent—as it does not replace the translated text or become its substitute.

Maybe this is what explains the appearance of bilingual editions. This is also probably what explains the absence of these editions in our culture. Here, I mean the absence of those 'mirror publications' which, from the beginning, put in front of their readers the text and its translation—the original and its copy—face to face, recognizing the transparency of the copy and its obligatory and permanent reference to the original text. These mirror publications urge the reader to produce and generate a third text through comparing and wedding the two texts to each other.

12 Quoted in Antoine Berman, *L'épreuve de l'étranger* (Paris: Gallimard, 1995), p. 97.

Like all contracts, this one respects the two parties involved. That is to say, it anchors foreignness at the same time that it produces proximity. This is because originals, even if they survive and achieve eternity, quickly enter the infinite process of renewing, transforming and foreignizing themselves.

Strangeness and transformation infuse new life into the translated text, transforming, renewing and inserting it into a new network of relations. It also opens it up to cultures within which it did not expect to live. On the occasion of the appearance of the English translation of one of Schiller's plays, Goethe wrote:

> The translator does not render a service only for his nation, but also for the nation from whose language he takes the work. For it happens that a nation draws vigour and strength from a work and absorbs it so fully into its interior life, that it becomes impossible to enjoy it, nor to draw pleasure from it. This concerns the Germans who quickly gulp down all books that are offered to them and, by too frequent repetitions of something they like, they destroy some of its qualities. Hence, no wonder that their own proper books appear to them fresh and revived as a result of an excellent translation.[13]

Goethe himself expresses this feeling after reading a Latin translation of one of his poems:

> For many years, I have not read this poem that I cherish among all my poems. Now I contemplate it as if I were contemplating a mirror, which, as we know, has a mighty magical force. Here, I see my feeling and my poetry, at once identical and transformed, inhabiting a more perfect language. I realize that Latin tends towards the concept and transforms what, in German, is dissimulated in an innocent way.[14]

In this dense text, Goethe points not only to the potential of translation and its great mirror-like capacity to transform and generate the simulacra, but also to the dialectical nature that characterizes all translations. The difference that Goethe makes here between German and Latin—between the thought that considers nature as modesty, masquerade and concealment, and the

---

13 Quoted in Fritz Strich, *Goethe und die Weltliteratur* (Bern: Franck Verlag, 1946), p. 36; quoted in Berman, *L'épreuve de l'étranger*, p. 107.

14 Quoted in Berman, *L'épreuve de l'étranger*, p. 106.

thought that tends towards concepts and clarity—lies in between any translation and even characterizes the acts of generating meanings. Any translation is a violent dialectic between the German spirit and the Latin spirit; between the synthetic thought—for which meaning is the fruit of effort, fight and violence—and the analytic thought, which achieves meaning in its presence and clarity; between the thought that sees misunderstanding as the basis of meaning's existence and achieves significations only by following tortuous and steep paths, and the thought that discovers them in the clear light of morning.

This struggle and violence inevitably break the mirror of translation. We find ourselves not in front of an original and a copy, but in front of a game of mirrors in which the original becomes a copy and the self becomes an other, and the transformation that affects the other quickly affects the self itself. This game of mirrors reveals that the self is distant from itself, and that it is an *other* in relation to itself.

This is because in its transformation of the translated text, translation transforms the translated language as well. In this context, one of the German theorists, Rudolf Pannwitz, wrote:

> Our translations, even the best ones, proceed from a mistaken premise. They want to turn Hindi, Greek, English into German instead of turning German into Hindi, Greek, English. Our translators have a far greater reverence for the usage of their own language than for the spirit of the foreign works [. . .] The basic error of the translator is that he preserves the state in which his own language happens to be instead of allowing his language to be powerfully affected by the foreign tongue.[15]

Maybe this is what explains the traces of French and English that we detect today in our Arabic texts—even in those that are not translated. For the translator, according to Benjamin, is called 'to break the decayed barriers of his own language'.[16] Translation, therefore, guarantees not only the life of the text and its transformation, development and proliferation, but also the life of language and thought.

15 Benjamin, 'Task of the Translator', pp. 261–62; 'La tâche du traducteur', p. 258.

16 Benjamin, 'Task of the Translator', p. 261; 'La tâche du traducteur', p. 259.

To introduce a French translation of one of his books, Heidegger argued that by translation, the work of thought finds itself donning the spirit of another language and undergoes an inevitable transformation. But this translation can be fecund because it raises the fundamental question in a new light.[17]

Heidegger wrote this introduction in 1932, that is, a few years before the publication of the first novel of Jean-Paul Sartre. He anticipated the fecundity and the resurgence that his thought would undergo through his French translations, and also the life that German philosophy would find in French thought. He confirmed by this that the most prosperous eras of thought necessarily coincide with the prosperity of translation movements. For translation is never a sign of subalternity. It is neither a suppression of the other nor a submission to him. Rather, it is transformation, renewal, nomadism, openmindedness, cross-pollination, proliferation and life.

17 Heidegger, *Questions I et II*, p. 10.

7
The Task of Translation, the Task of Thought

Undoubtedly, the reader has noticed that the above title refers to two famous texts: 'The Task of the Translator' by Walter Benjamin and 'The End of Philosophy and the Task of Thinking' by Martin Heidegger. These two great philosophers influence the subject we are treating, the thought we are discussing, and also the author in question, namely, Maurice Blanchot.

We should emphasize that the question here is not a secondary or marginal one—if the distinction between 'marginal' and 'central' has any meaning in this context. The question of translation places us at the core of Blanchot's intellectual preoccupations, if not to say at the core of his thought. This is what he himself confirms:

> and if one continues to say, rightly or wrongly, Here are the poets, and there the novelists, indeed the critics, all of whom are responsible for the meaning of literature, then one must in the same way count the translators, writers of the rarest sort and truly incomparable.[1]

We will discuss the question of translation in Blanchot's oeuvre through two essential texts. The first was published in the book *The Work of Fire*, under the title 'Translated from . . . ' and the second in *Friendship* under the title 'Translating'. In the latter text, Blanchot brings up the question of translation, commenting on Walter Benjamin's 'The Task of the Translator'. This, as we know, is Blanchot's habit, for his essays usually enter into a dialogue with a certain intellectual or critical review of a book.

In this regard, I would like to insist on a methodological issue that seems to me essential: it would be a hopeless, useless and perhaps meaningless attempt to distinguish between what belongs to Blanchot and what belongs to others—and, regarding the text in question, between what belongs to

1 Maurice Blanchot, 'Translating' in *Friendship* (Elizabeth Rottenberg trans.) (Stanford, CA: Stanford University Press, 1997), p. 57. Maurice Blanchot, 'Traduire' in *L'amitié* (Paris: Gallimard, 1971), p. 69.

Blanchot and what belongs to Benjamin. And this can, for many reasons, place us at the core of Blanchot's thought and, perhaps, determine his method of reading.

The question here is not renewing the utterance, but rather retelling it in a different way. Let us remember Blanchot's expression in his book *The Infinite Conversation*: 'what is important is not to tell, but to tell once again, and in this telling, to tell again each time a first time.'[2]

More precisely, it is a question of engaging in *un entretien infini* (infinite conversation) with what was already said. I use this term in its original version in order to draw attention to the fact that we make a mistake in translating it as *ḥiwār lā mutanāhī* For, as we know, the term *l'entretien* refers, above all, to *iḥtifāẓ wa-l-ṣiyāna* (preservation and maintenance). In this context, I prefer to say that it refers to *al-ʿināya wa-l-riʿāya* (care and upkeeping) more than to *al-ḥiwār* (conversation). Littré, in his dictionary, gives it the meaning of *ḥiwār* only when it is used in the plural to refer to the titles of books.

To clarify Blanchot's position further, we have to list some differences between him and the deconstructionist Jacques Derrida. While we feel with Derrida a sort of triumph over the read text, we feel with Blanchot a sort of intellectual modesty and a sense that there is always a voice that preceded us, that the question of thought is a quarrel between lovers. The matter is a question of care and infinite upkeeping of what has been said.

To retrieve what has been said does not mean to be content with explanations and commentaries. It rather means to accept that we find ourselves not before a reiterated and redundant identical, but before the same thing—before a diverse speech that does not cease to circulate back to us in the obscure clarity of what has been said. This caring, this upkeeping, is the task of thought, which imposes on it a kind of identification with intellectuals from a position of difference and otherness. It is also 'the task of the translator', as we will see.

Keeping what has already been said primarily means achieving the same thing that was said in different modes. As such, Blanchot confirms that the

---

2 Maurice Blanchot, *The Infinite Conversation* (Susan Hanson trans.) (Minneapolis, MN: University of Minnesota Press, 1993), p. 314. Maurice Blanchot, *L'Entretien infini* (Paris: Gallimard: 1969), p. 459.

task of the translator involves a sort of demonic work and a sort of disobedience: the disobedience of God. For the translator pretends to rebuild the Tower of Babel in order to 'elevate' to a sort of original language and most perfect speech—the speaking of which is sufficient to say the truth. The translator always has a dream that all languages indicate the same reality in different modes, as if he refers, by translation, to an ideal language that is probably the harmony or the complementary unity between all these modes.

This unifying aim does not mean that translation tends to eliminate difference. 'It alludes to it constantly; it dissimulates this difference, but occasionally in revealing it and often in accentuating it.'[3] Blanchot sees that the text, as such, has a sort of dynamism and a desire to get out of itself and to change its territory and its language. It is perhaps the characteristic of literary works as such. These are the works in which language reveals its future, undiscovered possibilities. It is in these works that language reveals its aspiration to get out of itself. We can say that translation 'exploits' this dynamism, profits from this aspiration—or, perhaps, uses it.

Blanchot believes that the so-called classical texts crystallize this question perfectly, for these texts often belong to dead languages, and they live only in and by their translations. They are at the same time 'the sole depositories of the life of a dead language and the only ones responsible for the future of a language that has no future.'[4]

Some littérateurs are interested in translation only to consecrate this dynamism—this departure from the norm and this alienation from tautological language. They come to translation precisely to live the experience of exile. In this context, Blanchot draws attention to the reason for the adherence in French classical literature to ancient cultures and languages, seeking the expatriation that aims to elevate the ordinary language to the level of the translated language. 'To transpose a Greek or Latin work into French,' said Blanchot, 'was enough to accomplish the essential part of a creative act. [. . .] In the preface to *Oedipus*, Corneille regrets having lost the advantage of being only a translator. The moderns assuredly go further. *Translated from Silence*, that work by Joe Bousquet, is like the wish of an entire literature that would

3 Blanchot, 'Translating' in *Friendship*, pp. 58–59; 'Traduire' in *L'Amitié*, pp. 70–71.

4 Blanchot, 'Translating' in *Friendship*, p. 59; 'Traduire' in *L'Amitié*, p. 71.

like to remain a translation in its pure state, an unburdened translation of something to be translated, an effort to retain, of language the only distance that language seeks to keep with regards to itself and that must, if pushed, result in its disappearance.'[5]

In this sense, the translator is a creative author, and the translated text mimics the process of creation, which attempts, from the ordinary language in which we live and are immersed, 'to give life to another language that seems to be the same language, though constituting its absence and difference, a difference which is perpetually acquired and constantly hidden.'[6]

Hence, translation does not aim to be a 'faithful' imitation, because imitation 'tends to unmake the work of translation, insofar as it acclimates it and thus takes away from it the privilege of the ambiguity, of the instability that make so many great translated works extraordinary.'[7]

The translator does not seek to eliminate difference, but to exploit it and preserve it. From this point of view, translation should not be essentially considered an act that engenders proximity, but rather an activity that anchors foreignness. The fundamental error the translator could make is to attempt the conservation of the contingent state of his own language, instead of subjecting it to the powerful action of the foreign language.

In this context, Blanchot invokes one of the German theorists of translation that Benjamin also quoted. This is what Rudolf Pannwitz writes: 'Our translations, even the best ones, proceed from a mistaken premise. They want to turn Hindi, Greek, English into German instead of turning German into Hindi, Greek, English.'[8]

This infinite opening to strangeness in all its forms does not facilitate the task of the translator, but rather overburdens him with a hard responsibility—which is, maybe, the same responsibility imposed on any intellectual work. Since the translator starts from the principle that any language may become all languages, he is obliged, in order to realize this, to be a creator in his own language; that is to say, to maintain the difference of his language

5 Blanchot, 'Translated From', p. 177; 'Traduit de', p. 174.

6 Blanchot, 'Translated From', p. 190 [translation modified]; 'Traduit de', pp. 186–87.

7 Blanchot, 'Translated From', p. 180; 'Traduit de', p. 177.

8 Benjamin, 'Task of the Translator', pp. 261–62.

from other languages, but also, and maybe essentially, the difference of his own language from itself . . .

At the heart of difference lives identity; and at the core of any exodus and movement resides stability and civilization. In the power of separation and the creation of distance, there is always the power of irredentism and assembling; at the heart of linguistic work, there is always intellectual work; and in the task of translation, there is the task of thought, as the two tasks become the same work.

Numerous are the great thinkers for whom the task of rethinking was blended with the task of retranslation. Hölderlin was one of the most prominent—if not the absolutely strongest—of these thinkers. Blanchot wrote:

> The example of Hölderlin illustrates the risk that is run, in the end, by the man fascinated by the power of translating: the translations of *Antigone* and *Oedipus* were nearly his last works at the outbreak of madness. These works are exceptionally studied, restrained, and intentional, conducted with inflexible firmness with the intent not of transposing the Greek text into German, nor of reconveying the German language to its Greek sources, but of unifying the two powers—the one representing the vicissitudes of the West, the other those of the Orient—in the simplicity of a pure and toral language. The result is almost frightful. It is as if one were discovering between the two languages an understanding so profound, a harmony so fundamental, that it substitutes itself for meaning, or succeeds in turning the hiatus that lies open between the two languages into the origin of a new meaning.[9]

9 Blanchot, 'Translating' in *Friendship*, p. 61; 'Traduire' in *L'Amitié*, p. 73.

8
The Revival of Poetry

Perhaps the best way to inaugurate this Moroccan–German encounter about translation and the modernization of poetry is to begin our talk with this poem by the great German poet, Goethe:

I PICKED a rustic nosegay lately,
And bore it homewards, musing greatly;
When, heated by my hand, I found
The heads all drooping tow'rd the ground.
I plac'd them in a well-cool'd glass,
And what a wonder came to pass
The heads soon raised themselves once more.
The stalks were blooming as before,
And all were in as good a case
As when they left their native place.

* * *

So felt I, when I wond'ring heard
My song to foreign tongues transferr'd

Translated by Edgar Alfred Bowring

Ein Gleichniß
Jüngst pflückt ich einen
Wiesenstrauß,
Trug ihn gedankenvoll nach Haus;

This paper was presented during a meeting with some German poets in a conference jointly organized by the departments of Arabic and German language in the Faculty of Letters of Mohammed V University, Rabat, in 1999.

Da hatten, von der warmen Hand, Die Kronen sich alle zur Erde gewandt.
Ich setzte sie in frisches Glas,
Und welch ein Wunder war mir das!
Die Köpfchen hoben sich empor,
Die Blätterstengel im grünen Flor,
Und allzusammen so gesund,
Als ständen sie noch auf Muttergrund

* * *

So war mir's, als ich wundersam
Mein Lied in fremder Sprache vernahm

Johann Wolfgang von Goethe (1828)

The title of this poem, 'An Emblem' ('Ein Gleichniß'), is itself emblematic: its author is an emblem; and it is in and of itself an emblem—an emblem of this encounter where each one of us aims to plant his flowers in other nurseries, to listen to one's poems in another language, to see one's self in the mirror of the other, and to enrich one's self by the other. Of course, Goethe is the only emblem that an encounter like this can focus on, because he is, above all, the first one that the Arab reader recognized—not as a cultural institute, but as one of Germany's greatest poets and intellectuals. Goethe, above all, because he was a bridge between the Orient and the Occident, and the author of the *West-östlicher Divan* (West-East Divan). He is, in fact, the occidental divan for the oriental reader.

Goethe was also one of the greatest theorists of translation—and maybe the first one who felt its importance not merely in the process of opening up to the other, but rather in the perception of the self.

One of the French historians of translation theory recounts the anecdote that in 1808, in the midst of the Napoleonic occupation of Germany, certain intellectuals wanted to make for the German people a useful collection of the best German poems. The nationalist intention of this work was known. The authors of the collection asked Goethe to advise them about the choice of poems. His sole advice for them was to include also the German translations of foreign poems, because German poetry was, since its birth, indebted in all its forms to the foreigner—and also because these translations, according to him, constitute creations that are inseparable from German literature.[1]

Perhaps this is exactly what Goethe means when he says that translation is an instrument to construct universality. He does not mean by this that national literature has enough room to contain foreign literatures. What he means by *Weltliteratur* (world literature) is neither the entirety of previous and present literatures, which an encyclopaedic vision can make available, nor all the great works that were able to rise to the level of universality and become the heritage of civilized humanity. *Weltliteratur* is a historical concept that concerns the recent relationship between different national literatures. The era of world literature is the one in which literatures are not content with their interaction with each other, but rather understand their existence within a framework of interaction which does not cease to increase.

The concept of *Weltliteratur* involves an idea about the self and the other, and subsequently, an idea about translation—where the latter becomes an instrument. Goethe does not advocate the modernization of poetry, but rather to refresh it, revive it, and regenerate it—*Auffrischung*. Though the notion of refreshment has nothing to do with our actual concept of modernization, just as world literature has nothing to do with globalized literature. However, we cannot deny that its effect on literature is not far from what we mean by the effect of modernization: a dissociation of the self from itself, and the departure of literature from itself and its cultivation outside its original place. For 'the exhausted national literature is revitalized and regenerated by the Other'.[2]

Revitalization is not only a resurrection and a new renaissance, but also a reconstruction of the self, a revision of the national and the universal. It is also a transformation, abrogation and dissolution. It is, according to Goethe, *metempsychosis*: 'the best metempsychosis is the one in which we see ourselves resurrected in another.'[3] This metempsychosis and this revitalization make

1 Berman, *L'épreuve de l'étranger*, pp. 94–95.

2 Berman, *L'épreuve de l'étranger*, p. 106.

3 Berman, *L'épreuve de l'étranger*, p. 106.

literature see itself in other literatures and in other languages—but they make it see itself in a different way: with other lives resurrected in it, inserted in other networks of relations and opened to cultures in which it never expected to live.

On the occasion of the appearance of the English translation of Schiller's play *Wallenstein*, Goethe wrote:

> The translator does not render a service only for his nation, but also for the nation from whose language he takes the work. For it happens that a nation draws vigour and strength from a work and absorbs it so fully into its interior life, that it becomes impossible to enjoy it, nor to draw pleasure from it. This concerns the Germans who quickly gulp down all books that are offered to them and, by too frequent repetitions of something they like, they destroy some of its qualities. Hence, no wonder that their own proper books appear to them fresh and revived as a result of an excellent translation.[4]

This feeling is expressed by Goethe himself after reading a Latin translation of one of his poems:

> For many years, I have not read this poem that I cherish among all my poems. Now I contemplate it as if I were contemplating a mirror, which, as we know, has a mighty magical force. Here, I see my feeling and my poetry, at once identical and transformed, inhabiting a more perfect language. I realize that Latin tends towards the concept and transforms what, in German, is dissimulated in an innocent way.[5]

Latin, which leans towards the concept and clarity, cultivates analytical thought and achieves significations in their presence and transparency. It refreshes German, which cultivates synthetic thought, makes significations ambiguous or difficult, and considers nature as prudishness, camouflage, and concealment.

What will contemporary Arabic do with the German poem? What will become of the German text once it is 'revived' in Arabic? On the other hand, what is the effect of the German translation on Arabic? What is the effect of

4 Berman, *L'épreuve de l'étranger*, p. 107.

5 Berman, *L'épreuve de l'étranger*, p. 106.

German poetry on the Arabic poem, which is said to enter modernity only through translation—to the extent that one scholar revealed that behind every modern Arab poet there is a foreign poet: behind al-Sayyāb, there is Edith Sitwell; behind Adonis, there is Saint-John Perse—not to mention the poets who exerted a great influence over modern Arabic poetry, such as T. S. Eliot and García Lorca.

What are the limits of this claim? What are the effects of translation here and there?

9

The Migration of the Philosophical Text

The term *hijra* (migration) refers us to the terms *naqla*, *naql* and *intiqāl*, derived from *naqala*, which means to transfer, remove, transport, transform and translate. These are terms which, as we know, were used to signify the meaning of translation. The French term *translation* was used until the end of the fourteenth century to indicate the same meaning.

What concerns us here is the translation movements experienced by philosophical texts. By the examination of translations into Arabic of philosophical texts, we may be able to determine the relations that linked—and are still linking—our Arabic philosophy with its other, especially in two essential moments of its history.

Let us first ask: What is the relation that classical Arabic philosophy established with the texts it translated? We will look for the answer to this question in two crucial texts. The first is extracted from the famous Munāẓara (Debate), recorded by Abū Ḥayyān al-Tawḥīdī in the *Kitāb al-imtāʿ wa-l-muʾānasa* (The Book of Delight and Conviviality), which took place between the logician Mattā Ibn Yūnus and the grammarian Abū Saʿīd al-Sīrāfī; the second is taken from al-Jāḥiẓ's work *Kitāb al-Ḥayawān* (The Book of Animals).

We read in the text of the *Munāẓara*:

ABŪ SAʿĪD AL-SĪRĀFĪ: So, you are not inviting us to know logic, but to learn Greek—though you yourself do not know it. How could you invite us to learn a language that you don't know, a language that went extinct a long time ago, and whose native speakers, who used it in their negotiations and communication, are dead, while you yourself translate from Syriac? What can you say about meanings that are transformed by transference from Greek to Syriac, and then from Syriac to Arabic?

MATTĀ: Even though the Greeks and their language have died, translation preserved the themes, communicated the meanings and rendered the truth.

ABŪ SAʿĪD: If we agree with you that the translation was accurate and that it never erred, [. . .] it is as if you are saying that the only logic is that of the Greeks, that the only argument is what they formulated, and that the only truth is what they revealed.

MATTĀ: No, but among all the nations, the Greeks are the keepers of wisdom, and thanks to their care, diverse sciences appeared and proliferated. We do not find this in other nations.

ABŪ SAʿĪD: You are wrong; you are bigoted and have surrendered to passion, for the omniscient's knowledge is spread all over the world and among all those who live in it.[1]

This text poses all the problems that the migration of philosophical texts encountered in classical Arabic culture—such as the plurality of the media of linguistic communication, the transformation caused by translation in the translated text, the doubt about the importance of openness to the culture of a unique other and the fear of submitting to the other and being partial to its culture.

Before we return to these issues in detail and ask whether we still face some of them, let us read the second extract, which we quote from al-Jāḥiẓ's famous text on translation:

> Translation transferred Indian books, translated Greek wisdom and transformed Persian literature. Some of them became more beautiful, and others lost nothing in their quality. If Arab wisdom (poetry) were to be translated, the inimitability that is the *wazn* (metre) would be lost, and if the *ʿajam* (non-Arabs) translated this wisdom, they would find that all that is said in it has already been mentioned in their own books, which were compiled for their understanding and wisdom.[2]

The fundamental meaning of this text is not that poetry is untranslatable, as is often claimed, but rather that the non-Arabs are not in need of the translation of Arabic poetry, Arabic texts or Arab wisdom, according to al-Jāḥiẓ.

---

1 Abū Ḥayyān al-Tawḥīdī, *Kitāb al-imtāʿ wa-l-muʾānasa* (Ahmed Amin et al. eds) (Beirut: Al Maktaba Al Messriyya, 1953), p. 116.

2 Al- Jāḥiẓ, *Kitāb al-Ḥayawān*, pp. 75–79.

The Arabic text does not need to be translated. Al-Jāḥiẓ could not imagine a translation from Arabic into another language. The only possible translation is the one done in the opposite direction—for Arabic is the language of culture. Therefore, when the literature of the Persians, the books of the Indians and the wisdom of the Greeks are translated, they are elevated and become more beautiful, or at least lose nothing. So, there is no need to retranslate them.

Perhaps this is what explains why our ancient philosophers did not feel, at all, the need to establish a link between reinterpreting and exegesis, or between retranslation and returning once again to the originals. Today, it is hard for us to understand why they did not feel, when reading Aristotle, the necessity to retranslate his work—unlike what we observe today with the great intellectuals who place great importance on the connection between interpretation and retranslation, or at least on the revision and correction of a translation. Let us remember Heidegger as a reader of the pre-Socratics, Althusser as a reader of Feuerbach and Marx, and Derrida as a reader of Hegel, Nietzsche and Freud.

Before inquiring about the reason why our ancients did not feel this need, let us first see whether what we have said is applicable to our modern philosophers. It is clear that our situation today is different, and that the relation we have with Western philosophical texts is not the same as the one our ancestors had with the texts they translated. It seems that we are obsessed with the incessant return to the originals that we translate, and with the permanent revision of what we translate, despite its scarcity. The evidence for this is the presence of multiple Arabic translations for the same text. A scholar has counted seven translations that successively appeared for the same work. Besides, we know, for instance, that we have more than one translation of Descartes's *Discourse on the Method* and *Meditations*.

Yet, is the existence of some particular cases sufficient to conclude that the relation we have today with Western philosophy is totally different from the one our ancestors had with their others? To answer this question, it might be necessary to distinguish between two types of diversity in translations.

There is what we may call a sporadic pluralism, and what we may call an abrogative pluralism. The example I can use to illustrate this second type of pluralism is the one that marked, and still marks, the relation that French philosophy has had—and continues to have—with the German texts it translated. We all know that the great contemporary French philosophers are translators of German texts, but what is remarkable in their translations is that they abrogate one another. The phenomenon that characterizes the French translation movement is reconsideration. This applies not only to texts that are known for their difficulty, such as those of Heidegger, but also to the works of Nietzsche, Freud, Husserl and Hegel. Since the beginning of the transfer of their works into French, they have been translated and retranslated. There is a permanent return to the original text, and the most important thing is that this return takes the form of revision and reconsideration.

It is as if the German text has to migrate in order to survive in its successive translations, and translation here becomes a kind of intellectual investment. Between the current French translations of Nietzsche and those that began in the 1940s, there is both a temporal and an intellectual distance. This is also the case for the translations of Freud, Marx and Hegel.

Great books, as they are, benefit from a sort of dynamism and a desire to get out of themselves—to change their original territory, to change their attire, and to transform their language. These texts have an infinite desire for migration. Language, in these texts, reveals the future potential it conceals, as well as its aspiration to get out of itself. We can say that translation exploits this dynamism and invests in this aspiration—or let us just say that it utilizes it.

I do not think we can say that the way we practise translation today exploits this dimension. I also do not think we can apply what we have just said about French translations to our current translations of the texts that we have transferred—and continue to transfer. These translations are rare, and even when they are multiple translations of the same text, there are no intellectual distances, and perhaps no temporal distances between them. We notice that these translations succeed one another, but they do not interact with each other, nor with the transferred texts and the translated thought. There is no real investment and no intellectual appropriation of the translated text.

What proves this are certain philosophical texts that were translated long ago into Arabic—such as Nietzsche's *Zarathustra*, Spinoza's *Treatise*, Wittgenstein's *Tractatus* and a few by Freud and Locke. These texts were Arabized without having any extension, without attracting attention, without raising problems or entering into new networks of relations. That is to say, they did not enter into a dialogue with Arabic culture—as if they were transferred to Arabic without being truly translated into it.

Can we conclude from this that the relation we now have with the texts we translate is not fundamentally different from the one our ancestors had with the texts they translated?

One important thing that should be emphasized here is that this apparent similarity conceals an essential difference between the two historical moments. Here, I mean the difference between the relations of power that linked classical Arabic culture to its other, and those which we have today with the other. Classical culture used to consider Arabic as the language of culture. Therefore, a text became more beautiful—or at least lost nothing—when it was translated into Arabic, as al-Jāḥiẓ says. No wonder then that Arabic translations were later used as original texts—or even as origins. It is sufficient to remember, for example, that the Arabic translation of *Kalīla wa-Dimna* was used as the original source for Latin, English and French translations, and even for the modern Persian translation, as one scholar has affirmed.[3]

The relation of power that links us today—or more precisely, links the Arabic language and thought—with the texts of others is different from and opposed to this earlier relation, if not completely reversed. We do not feel that we promote the text or add to its beauty when we translate it into Arabic. On the contrary, we feel that it is our texts that become more beautiful when they are transferred to foreign languages. They improve when they are translated.

No wonder, then, that some of us show so much interest in the translation of our works into other languages—as if we write only to be translated, just as we translate only in order to write. Some of our Arab writers even resort, after writing in a foreign language, to translating what they have written. One critic points out that some Arab novelists think of their probable translator while writing. They create their works guided by potential translation: 'They work hard to facilitate the task of the translator by avoiding the use of expressions and references that might not fit the style of another language.'[4]

3 Mohammed Abed al-Jabri, *al-ʿAql al-akhlāqī al-ʿArabī* (Casablanca/Beirut: Arabic Cultural Centre, 2001).

4 Kilito, *Lan tatakallam lughatī*, p. 25.

They usually wait for the appearance of the translation of what they have written, and it is only at this moment that they feel the value of their works.

We understand the meaning and significance of this when we know that a writer such as al-Jāḥiẓ, a poet such as al-Mutanabbī, or a philosopher like Ibn Rushd never worked on the translation of their books into a language other than Arabic, and never hoped for, predicted, or even imagined such translations. Our creative writing now happens in light of translation, as if the originals are effects of their translations. Even if it is necessary to talk about betrayal, we should say with Borges that 'the original is unfaithful to the translation'.[5]

This situation, which I am content to describe as different from the previous one, allows neither a productive treatment of foreign texts nor an effective translation of them. Even worse, it prevents any productive usage of Arabic texts themselves.

In this case, we cannot establish this productive relationship unless we reverse the relations of power that link us with the other. This, of course, can happen only if we truly appropriate its thought—that is, if we free ourselves from the other. For appropriation in the domain of thought does not mean conversion or closeness, but rather remoteness, the creation of distance and the production of questions.

This means that we cannot establish an Arabic philosophical thought unless we create translations that eliminate the metaphysics of translation. I do not mean translations that set themselves free from the notion of the original text, but rather those translations that set themselves free from the desire to be transformed into original texts. That is, translations that do not cease to adhere to their originals and to revise themselves; dialogic translations that advance the text, reproduce it and recognize the permanent need to return to the originals and become familiar with them; translations that do not aim to eliminate difference, but rather to utilize and foster it; translations that do not intend to create kinship, but to consecrate strangeness; translations that revive thought, transform it, blaze new paths for it, open new horizons for it and allow texts to remain and survive as they fly and migrate.

5 Borges, *Enquetes 1937–1952*, pp. 201–202.

10
Translation as a Tool for Modernization

By modernization, we do not mean here a social movement which affects institutions, changes situations and transforms structures, but rather a position on being and a conception of time. If we accept the premise that tradition is the situation in which contact constitutes the weft of being, and the link is the tissue of time—in other words, the situation in which major issues are raised in relation to the exploration of continuity and permanence: the permanence of identities that define, qualities that characterize and features that distinguish the language that we speak, the customs with which we are familiar, the realities we believe in, the expressions we constantly repeat and the ideas we circulate—if we assume that tradition refers to all this, then modernization can only be a persistent process of separation that puts the logic of continuity under question, makes of identity an infinite process of annexation and spacing and makes of the other an open sphere for difference and agreement.

Conceived in this way, the issue that we want to discuss here can be formulated as follows: How should translation be understood and practised in order to be a tool for modernization and separation? How can translation be a means of contributing to the discombobulation and transformation that our culture witnesses in a world in which cultures interact in an unprecedented manner? How can translation be a tool that permits culture to be separated from itself and to be opened to different cultures, a tool that permits language to be separated from itself and be opened to plurality, and a tool that permits the transformation of identity and opens it to the exterior? In brief, how can translation be a tool to consecrate strangeness?

It is evident that the ethical and metaphysical atmosphere in which we are used to posing the issues of translation, and in which we link them to a philosophy of identity and difference and a certain theory of writing and language, prevents translation from being a tool for modernization. This atmosphere makes translation essentially a tool to create kinship, deny difference and consecrate continuity.

We usually consider translation successful only if it is able to eliminate cultural and linguistic differences and transfer the text from one language to another without giving the impression of it being translated. We consider translation successful only if the translated text looks like 'a copy conformed to the original', as if 'it has not been translated', and as if it speaks 'our' language, expresses 'our' personality, and belongs to 'our' culture. We hope that the translated text reaches a degree in which it appears similar to the one the author would reach if he wrote his text in the translating language. We ask the translator to write the text in the name of its author, to write it without signing it and to remove his name in order to permit the writer of the original text to speak another language without losing his identity.

It is a translation that seeks to suppress the distance between the translator and the author, and to cancel the difference between the original language and the translated language. It is also a translation that hopes that the effect of the translated text on the new reader is the same as the effect produced on the reader of the original text.

It is, then, a translation that denies itself as a translation and seeks to produce a text that seems 'as if it has not been translated'—a text that erases the act of translation, a text where we do not find the trace of the foreign language, the trace of the 'foreigner', the trace of strangeness, the trace of change, the trace of otherness and the trace of difference.

Of course, we are not trying here to give a readymade recipe for what can be an alternative to this conception of translation, but we will do our best to deconstruct this metaphysics of translation. To accomplish this, let us first stop at its postulates.

This position posits that texts remain inviolable identities unless translation forces them to escape themselves and open to the other. This position also assumes that language remains unique and unified until translation befalls it to undermine the Tower of Babel and impose plurality on it. It also assumes that writing does not contain any self-strangeness, and that texts are not fundamentally threatened by strangeness in their 'own home'. So, what if language is essentially the home of difference and the shelter of plurality? And what if the original text itself contains its opposite? What if writing itself is an act that introduces strangeness into the mother tongue?

Proust said: 'masterpieces always seem as if they were written in a foreign language.'[1] This means that language can ascend to a level where it is distanced and differentiated from itself, even before hosting another language and before it is 'transferred' by translation. Writing, Barthes states, is a 'betrayal of language', an equivocation and introduction of strangeness into what we are familiar with. It is a displacement of the culture and of the language that transfers it.

Moreover, does language wait for the act of translation—or rather the act of writing—in order to be diverse? Is it not true that any linguistic system conceals plurality within itself? We all live the experience of multilingualism within the same language. The majority of contemporary texts are written today in many languages: they cite many words and passages that are borrowed from different languages. In this sense, every original text contains a translation, or, rather, translations. It embraces the other and introduces difference to its identity. There are even texts that generally belong to the same language, but they are absent from the text although they are related to it. Any text, explicitly or implicitly, involves disparate texts. Any text is a plurality even if it remains an individual text; it is a difference even if it remains an identity; and it is a translation even if it is not translated.

Texts do not wait for translation to force them to leave themselves and be separated from themselves. They permanently long for difference and strangeness. Any great text has the benefit, as such, of desiring to be planted in a different soil, to change its homeland, and to alter its language. Maybe this is the characteristic of great works, such as they are. They are texts which circulate between cultures. It is in these texts where language reveals its desire to leave itself. We can say that translation exploits this dynamism and this desire. Translation, then, is a creation in another language, or more accurately a creation in a language—a creation that seeks, from the ordinary language in which we live and are submerged, to give birth to another language which seems to be the same language, but constitutes 'its absence and difference that is perpetually acquired and constantly hidden'.[2]

---

1 Marcel Proust, 'Préface de Bernard de Fallois' in *Contre Sainte-Beuve* (Paris: Gallimard, 1954).

2 Blanchot, 'Traduit de', p. 187.

For this reason, translation does not have to conform to the original text and reproduce it, but it has to permit it to transfer from one culture to another, and to remain and survive. In this regard, transfer would be meaningless without transition, and survival would have no meaning if it were not transformation, likewise for renewal, if it were not development, proliferation and profusion.

Translation is what opens culture, what opens texts to the exterior and what transports and transforms them. Due to this transformation, many books receive a certain importance which surprises the literature they used to belong to, and acquire certain characteristics that this literature would not recognize for them. Hence, Blanchot states: 'French readers are surprised by the influence exerted by their realist writers (particularly Maupassant) over foreign writers who seem to us a bit unrealistic. Therefore, we get astonished when we know that Flaubert was the mentor of Kafka.'[3]

However, we should not understand transformation here as unidirectional. Translation does not only transform the translated text, but, when it does, it transforms, at the same time, the translating language. This is maybe what explains the traces of Spanish, French, and English that we start to find today in our contemporary Arabic texts, even among those texts that are not translated.

Thus, translation has to be problematic and must not pretend to overcome all difficulties, erase all distances, or eliminate all differences. For it is inevitable that translation admits its defeat before what is untranslatable—before what testifies to strangeness, distance, and alterity, and finally before what refuses submission, annexation, and assimilation. This means that translation should recognize the other as another. In this regard, Goethe says:

> [W]e must not get into an immediate conflict with the foreign language. We must reach the untranslatable and respect it; for therein lies the value and character of every language [. . .]. In translation, we have to reach what is untranslatable, for only in this case do we become conscious of the foreign nation and the foreign language.[4]

---

3 Blanchot, 'Traduit de', p. 175.

4 Quoted in Berman, *L'épreuve de l'étranger*, p. 97.

This means that stopping at the untranslatable is not merely a confrontation with linguistic difficulties that denote the weakness and incompetence of the translator. It is not the translator who is weak and incompetent, but rather the language itself that stands unable before the other language; it is the culture itself that stands before the other culture. So, it is not a question of incapability, but rather a perception of the otherness of the other. This means that bridging the gap between languages, which is the aim of translation, is at the same time a distancing. This also means that translation, seeking to unify languages, creates, in the same way, difference between them, and even exacerbates this difference. Translation is not only kinship and familiarity, but also a consecration of strangeness. It is not only continuity, but also a separation and alienation. It approaches the self to the other, but it also separates them from one another, for the distance between the self and the other cannot be crossed out completely—and if it is excluded, there will be no self and no other.

Contrary to the view that the interaction between cultures and the transfer between languages means that one of the two dominates, obliterates, eliminates, and assimilates the other, there is another view: that culture has to be opened to the other culture by coming closer to it—but at a distance—and communicating with it in separation. Thereby, translation does not intend to make our Arabic language and culture 'digest' and Arabize foreign texts; rather, it also aims—maybe essentially—to enable our Arabic culture to be foreignized, Gallicized, Anglicized and Germanized. In this way, translation becomes an instrument that permits culture to test itself in the light of the other, the foreigner, and a means by which the self is put to the ordeal and the test, where it receives a violent impulsion from what is foreign. It is this impulsion that makes the self feel strange—not only before the other, but before itself as well. Hence, translation becomes a separation of culture from itself, of language from itself, and of the self from itself. It is only by this that translation becomes a generator of identity, a nourisher of culture, and a tool for both separation and modernization.

BOOK II

Hosting the Stranger

There is no incompatibility between the repetition and novelty of what differs. Tangentially and elliptically, a difference always deflects repetition. I call it 'itérabilité', the emergence of the other (Sanskrit, itara) in reiteration.

Jacques Derrida, 'Autrui est secret parce qu'il est autre'.

Introduction

Does the Original Dispense of Its Translations?

Bilingual publications seem unable to justify themselves. Who are they actually addressed to? If the reader does not master the original language, he will be content with the translation; but if he can read the text in its original language, he will then need no translation.

This objection will only be convincing to those who ignore the nature of the relationship between a text and its translation—or more accurately, its translations—which is a relationship defined by familiarity, or let us say by love and passion. If a translation clings to this convivance with its original 'version', it's because the copy has a ceaseless yearning to return to its original and see itself in its mirror. In fact, what characterizes the copy is its persistent feeling that it has not sufficiently acknowledged its debt to the original. In this sense, every translation, whatever its value, is always problematic.

It is maybe for this reason that Benjamin insists on many occasions that a translation does not replace the original. This does not mean that it remains constantly inferior to the original, but that it cannot exist without it. It never ceases to cling to it. If it is so, it's because the original is vitally in need of it, too. For every text, as Benjamin says, expresses 'the great longing for linguistic complementation. A real translation is transparent; it does not cover the original, does not block its light.'[1]

In this way, bilingual editions seem to be neither a publication of a text nor its translation, but rather an infinite transmission of a back and forth between an original and its copies. This type of edition does not address the reader who hasn't mastered the original language, nor does it address the one who ignores it. Rather, it addresses a reader who is invited to read a text between the two languages—a reader who is not concerned with the conformity of the copy to its original, but rather someone who is anxious to heighten the difference between what seems to be identical; a reader who is

1 Benjamin, 'Task of the Translator', p. 260; 'La tâche du traducteur', p. 257.

not enamoured with the creation of proximity, but rather eager to establish strangeness; a reader who is striving to generate a third text by combining the two texts and the two languages.

Perhaps it is this desire to generate problematics and to highlight gaps that made some scholars not content, in the wake of Benjamin, to argue that the copy does not replace its original—but that the original itself does not replace its translations either.

In this vein, Umberto Eco wrote, 'When I read a translation by a major poet of a poem by another major poet, it's because I know the original and I want to know what it became in the hands of the poet-translator.'[2] (This quote reminds me of the back-and-forth movements I had in high school between the 'original' version of Lamartine's 'Le Lac' [The Lake] and its Arabic translation 'al-Buḥayra' by Ali Mahmoud Taha.)

So, isn't it befitting, then, not to publish a text without its translations, and not to publish translations without their originals?

2 Umberto Eco, *Dire presque la même chose* (Paris: Grasset, 2006), p. 14.

1
On the Untranslatable

> The text lives only if it survives, and it survives only if it is, at the same time, translatable and untranslatable. Totally translatable: it disappears as a text, as writing, as a body of language. Totally untranslatable: even inside what is believed to be a language, it dies immediately.
>
> Jacques Derrida, *Parages*

> To descend into the untranslatable, to experience its shock without muffling it, until everything Occidental in us totters and the rights of the 'father tongue' vacillate.
>
> Roland Barthes, *The Empire of Signs*

There are two conceptions of translation, and each one results in a specific definition of the untranslatable.

The first conception affirms, from the start, that translation is possible but may encounter some difficulties that make it complicated—or even, in some cases, impossible; whereas the second, from the start, sees translation as difficult and impossible, but nonetheless necessary. It is an impossibility that must be braved, a difficulty that must be faced and overcome, a prohibition that must be transgressed.

While the first conception assumes that a potential mutual understanding and a primary rapprochement are possible, the second assumes an inherent misunderstanding, pluralism and a fundamental difference.

The first conception postulates that the possibility of translation is a given and that the impossibility is to be conquered, whereas the second conception sees the opposite. In the first conception, possibility is a principle and impossibility a finality, while in the second, impossibility is the starting point. Against the impossible possibility, there is the possibility of the impossible.

What does the *untranslatable* mean in both cases?

Before responding, it is necessary to recognize that this question, in relation to the two conceptions, does not take on the same importance—nor, perhaps, the same significance. The first conception hardly gives any importance to the untranslatable, since it places it outside the act of translating or at its margin. The untranslatable is the boundary where translation and its possibilities stop. It is *what cannot be translated*. On the other hand, the second conception, since it perceives translation as a conquest and a fight against an inseparable resistance, sees in the untranslatable the places where symptoms of difference between languages and cultures appear.

This doesn't mean that rapprochement is impossible, nor that what is untranslatable can never be translated, but rather that we do not cease to translate. The untranslatable, therefore, is not what cannot be translated, but what is infinitely translatable (*l'infiniment traduisible*).

This conception, therefore, gives crucial significance to what is untranslatable and fully implicates it in the act of translating. It perceives it as 'what we do not cease (not to) translate', according to the expression of Derrida.[1]

The use of the verb 'to cease' forces us to check our earlier definition of what we called a second conception. It seems that the impossibility of translation, according to this conception, is not only a simple principle; it is rather consubstantial with translation. It is what penetrates it and makes of the translatable the essence of the untranslatable. Let's also say that this conception deconstructs the translatable/untranslatable binary, that is, it causes the two terms to move away from each other through rapprochement.

If the first conception separates these two terms and throws the untranslatable out of the operation and away from the act of translating—privileging one over the other—the second conception, on the other hand, brings the two closer, the translatable and the untranslatable, and makes what must be translated precisely what is untranslatable: that is, what manifests refusal, resistance, stubbornness and strangeness.

Also, defining the untranslatable as what we do not cease to translate makes the act of translating an infinite openness and a perpetual tension. Perhaps this is the most important thing that distinguishes this conception

1 Derrida, 'Des tours de Babel'.

from the other. While the first conception proposes the act of translating within a closed temporality and a serene relationship, the second opens it to the future and makes of the translatable something perpetually dependent on the untranslatable. It also causes the text to live an endless life in its translations.

This second conception sees in the translation of what ceaselessly refuses translation successive triumphs (or defeats that are ceaselessly overcome), and a perpetual rediscovery of the translated text and the target language.

This conception implicitly recognizes the permanent need for the originals—to return to them and be familiar with them. It affirms that translation is a continuous creation, that it is a perpetual movement between the possible and the impossible, that it cannot be the other itself, that the text does not cease to cling to its translation, and that every translation remains transparent and neither excludes the translated text nor replaces it.

According to this conception, translation is what breathes life into texts and transmits them from one culture to another. The text lives only because it is at the same time translatable and untranslatable. If it were possible to make a final translation of a given text, then it would die—both as a text and as a piece of writing: For imitation 'tends to unmake the work of translation, insofar as it acclimates it and thus takes away from it the privilege of the ambiguity, of the instability that make so many great translated works extraordinary.'[2]

If translation tends to be final—to be a copy that conforms to the original and to make of the translating language a mirror that reflects the original text, decisive in determining what is translatable and what is untranslatable, separating them categorically and casting what is untranslatable outside the act of translating—then it would be using a unique kind of language, one which must necessarily change. The medium of translation is a living language, and its mirror is condemned to break. In this sense, the translator is a creator in another language—or more accurately, a creator in language. For that reason, it is not necessary for him to transmit the text and reproduce it, nor to communicate its original meaning, because translation has no relation to reporting and information. The role of the translator, as Benjamin observed,

2 Blanchot, 'Translated From', p. 180; 'Traduit de', p. 177.

is to permit the text to remain and survive—and this survival would not deserve the name if the translation were not a mutation and a renewal. The original text changes; that is, it develops and proliferates. The translations of a text are what constitute its 'history'—but a history that contains struggle and difference. The aim of what we have called the first conception is to reduce this (linguistic, cultural, and ideological) difference and transform it into a unity, as though the task of translation were not to find concordance but to revive differences. This task is neither replacement nor reconciliation, but rather a continuous act of thinking.

Perhaps the first conception denies this task because it starts from postulates, the most important of which is that language is merely a medium of communication, and that it is only a contingent garment which enables the transmission of compatible ideas through space and time.

If it is possible for us to speak and read a language, it is because, according to this conception, we understand it and understand each other by means of it. Translation, which signifies in this case finding equivalents between one language and another, is our tool for rapprochement and understanding. If we encounter difficulties, we attribute them to a lack of respect for grammar and inappropriate uses of meanings.

However, the status and role of translation change if we postulate that words are not a passive means of communication, that language is not only a medium of communication, and that it enjoys the ability to act, for it hides and reveals, divides and unites, dazzles and fascinates. Language is also transmitted through subjectivities that are transformed by the shift of times and places. For meanings cannot be ascribed to placid linguistic structures; translation necessarily involves the writing, the reading and the translating subjectivities in the midst of the acts of writing, reading and rereading, translating and retranslating.

In this way, the theoretical problem that the practice of translation poses does not concern the possible equivalence between one language and another. For the resistance and difficulty presupposed by what we have called the second conception is nothing but a symptom of what escapes language when it is not reduced to a mere medium of communication. It is the proof that what preoccupies the translator is not to connect and bring closer, nor to attract the other to the self and absorb it, but rather to move towards the other—to open the text, to open the culture to the otherness of the other, to enrich the text and the culture by fertilizing them with the other language and by 'hosting the stranger'.

It is inevitable that translation occurs between languages that are linked by relations of power. The weakness of the first conception lies in the fact that it does not recognize the power of these relations. It does not try to exploit this power and enter into a struggle with the foreign language—not to subdue it and exclude from texts all that refuses to submit and cast it into the circle of the untranslatable—but rather to problematize the act of translating. Translation here does not seek to stop at 'the untranslatable' and that which can attest to strangeness, distance and 'otherness'—and therefore also that which testifies to a deceptively simple refusal to surrender. Translation is not a strategy for generating differences. It rather opens the language to its 'exterior' and opens the stranger, as such, to the space of the translating language.

Goethe wrote: 'We have to examine what we feel towards the translated work and see to what extent this live power can evoke our strength and fertilize it.' The question here is to know, while translating, what is possible and to what limit we can push the target language. What flexibility does it allow, thanks to the fertilization that translation produces? The concept of 'fertilization' used here by Goethe indicates the degree to which translation makes language reveal untapped possibilities.

Translation, then, is not a transition from a stable semantic content to a different form of expression. It is rather a development and fertilization of meaning by means of another language which, through an act of intrinsic differentiation, reveals new possibilities. Far from being the effect of a lack of understanding (manque) which the translator tends to fill, translation is creativity whose starting point is the plurality and difference of languages. In this sense, Derrida illustrates that the translated work 'does not only live for so long, but also lasts longer and improves'. It survives beyond itself, and it survives beyond the capacities of its writer—and we can add: the capacities of its original language, the capacities of its text. Umberto Eco wrote, 'I felt how my text, in its contact with another language, exhibits interpretative potentials which remained hidden to me.'[3]

3 Eco, *Dire presque la même chose*, p. 14.

In this sense, translation becomes at once a curse and a blessing—it is *bene* and *mala diction*, according to Derrida's expression.[4] Undoubtedly, this requires us to reread the myth of Babel so as to see in it a call for translation, starting from plurality, dispersion, confusion and mixing, and also to consider translation as both impossible and necessary at the same time—and that it is exactly what makes the impossible possible. Translation here is similar to what some might expect from politics, in that it is 'an act which aims to make the impossible possible'.

In this way, the untranslatable becomes a part of translation, not what is found in its margin, on the threshold and limit of the possible, but rather what makes the act of translating necessary. Because the untranslatable exists, there is a necessity to translate. Impossibility exists only when there is demand and quest, and rejection exists only when there is an ardent desire, but desire exists only when resistance, refusal and opposition dominate.

4 Jacques Derrida, *Parages* (Paris: Galilée, 1986), p. 148.

2
Self-Translation: When the Author Translates His Work

> I felt how my text, in its contact with another language, exhibits interpretative potentials which remained hidden to me.
>
> Umberto Eco, *Dire presque la même chose*

I aim to broach the subject of translation through the analysis of a particular case, which may permit us to formulate a number of questions on the subject. I mean the case in which the author translates his own work—self-translation. We will take as an example Abdallah Laroui's translation of his own book *L'idéologie arabe contemporaine*, published in 1996 as *al-ʾIdiyūlūjiyā al-ʿarabiyya al-muʿāṣira.*[1] We will focus particularly on his introduction to this translation. It is an introduction that poses different issues, but we will deal only with those relevant to the question that concerns us here.

It is known that this 1996 translation by Laroui was not the first translation of *L'idéologie arabe contemporaine*. It was essentially done, as stated by the author-translator himself, to rectify a previous translation published in Beirut in 1970,[2] three years after the publication of the French version of the book in 1967. The more recent Arabic translation, whose introduction was penned by the author and is the topic of this essay, was published about thirty years after the French edition, and more than a quarter of a century after the first translation by Mohamed Itani.

---

1 Abdallah Laroui, *al-ʾĪdiyūlūjiyā al-ʿarabiyya al-muʿāṣira* (Casablanca: al-Markaz al-Thaqāfī al-ʿArabī, 1995). Originally written in French as *L'idéologie arabe contemporaine* (Maxime Rodinson pref.) (Paris: F. Maspero, 1967).

2 Abdallah Laroui, *al-ʾĪdiyūlūjiyā al-ʿarabiyya al-muʿāṣira* (Mohamed Itani trans.) (Beirut: Dar al-Ḥaqīqa, 1970).

Laroui starts his introduction by explaining the reasons that pushed him to conduct 'a new translation of my first book I published in French'. He attributes this retranslation to the numerous errors he discovered in the first translation, 145 in his own count.

The first thing that draws the attention of the reader of this introduction is that Laroui is not content to call his work 'a new translation', which rectifies the errors committed by the other translator, and he affirms that the reader, 'for the first time, will read the original version of the book'.[3]

The first question that arises here is: is it correct to call the work of the author-translator here—and really any self-translation—an original text? And in what sense?

Nothing seems to prohibit this, since the translator in this case is the author himself, who is supposed to be the one who best knows the secrets and nuances of his text. Basically, he is the one most able to understand the meanings of his words, the implications of his metaphors and the exact significations of his expressions. There is therefore no need for the author-translator to indulge in speculations in order to know the intentions of the author, nor to determine the profile of the readers he is addressing. He will translate only his ideas and what is already on his mind. He is more aware than anyone else of what the text said and what it didn't, what it emphasized and what it ignored.

We are dealing with a case where the mediations between the translator and the text to be translated seem almost non-existent or weakened, a case in which translation becomes a first writing. We can therefore say that it is a case where the copy becomes identical to the original, if not to say, with Laroui, that it is 'an original text'.

However, if we take into consideration the dates which I intentionally gave at the beginning, we will see that there is a temporal gap of thirty years between the translation made by the author and the French original version. So, if the lack of mediation is what pushed the author-translator to call the new translation an original text, there is at least a temporal gap, which is neither short nor meaningless. The author-translator himself is aware of its importance, especially for the issues the book raises and the concepts on which it is based, such as ideology, Marxism, liberalism and universalism.

3 Laroui, *al-ʾĪdiyūlūjiyā*, p. 14.

These concepts, as we know, have undergone essential transformations during the aforesaid era. Therefore, we read on page fifteen of the introduction (that is, the page following the one where the author calls his translation 'an original text'): 'But now, fascinating events have happened and their explanation has perplexed many people. Does that mean, however, that this has no effect on how the book should be read today?'[4]

This question posed by the author-translator applies to all readers, including the writer of the book. For Laroui, the translator, is also a reader of a book by Laroui, the author. He is a reader who is determined by a historicity that is completely different from that of the reader at the end of the sixties, who used the concepts of ideology, Marxism and universalism, and receives them in a totally different sense than the reader at the end of the nineties, after major events—not least of which was the fall of the Berlin Wall in 1989.

We cannot then affirm that the new translation is free of any mediation, even though it is accomplished by the author himself—for there is, at the very least, the mediation of time.

But there is another mediation which, as we know, exists in every translation: the mediation of the translating language, which makes every text, even if translated by its writer, shift from one language to another, from one cultural space to another, and address a different receiver. Even if the author of the text remains the same during translation, other variables certainly change. This may result in the escape of textual meanings from the control and authority of the author-translator. This is what Laroui notices with regard to the first translation, but he attributes this only to the errors of the translation—not to *the effects* of translation. He wonders how some 'theories were attributed to his book which in reality contradict it'. He argues, 'I later published several explanatory writings which could have been used to correct the shortcomings of the first translation, but this is the one which is used as a basis for interpreting later writings.'[5]

It is necessary to pay attention here to the author's confusion regarding what happened to his book when it was translated into another language, and also to his inability to resolve the situation. What is important here is not the transformation that occurred to the text, but rather the fact that the

4 Laroui, *al-ʾĪdiyūlūjiyā*, p. 15.

5 Laroui, *al-ʾĪdiyūlūjiyā*, p. 14.

translated text—*the effect* of translation—spreads and influences subsequent published texts, and is used as a basis for their interpretation. It is as if the author is unable to resolve what is happening to his book, to his writings, to what has been translated from them, and to what followed the translation. It is as if the author controls nothing and loses all his authority. This reveals that the transfer of the text to another language distances it even from its author and frees it from his control. This is probably the reason why the new translation is undertaken. This new translation does not aim merely to remedy 'language errors', but rather to contain the effects of the first translation—not only on the translated text, but also on the texts that followed it.

So, is it enough for the author to take charge of the translation of his own book in order to cancel these effects and control the situation? Is it enough to remove certain mediations or reduce them in order to rectify the situation and make the translated text adhere as closely as possible to the original text?

To answer all these questions, we can turn to a text cited by Laroui in this introduction. In his illustration of the importance of translation in the modernization of Arab thought, Laroui cites a passage by Abū Ḥayyān al-Tawḥīdī taken from the Munāẓara (debate), mentioned in the *Kitāb al-imtāʿ wa-l-muʾānasa*, featuring both the logician Mattā Ibn Younes and the grammarian Abou Saʿīd al-Sīrāfī. The latter asked: 'You who translate from Syriac, what can you say about meanings which are transformed by transference from Greek to Syriac, then from Syriac to Arabic?' Mattā Ibn Younes said: 'Even though the Greeks and their language died, translation preserved the themes, communicated the meanings and rendered the truth.' Abou Saʿīd al-Sīrāfī replied: 'If we agree with you that the translation was accurate and that it never erred—*even if this cannot be, because it is not in the nature of languages nor in the destiny of meanings*—it is as if you are saying that the only logic is that of the Greeks'[6]

This text uses two interpretations to clarify the shift in meanings and the distance of the copy from the original. The first emphasizes the linguistic and temporal mediation, and what calls 'the transformation by transposition from one language to another'. The second interpretation—though not clearly articulated in this passage—attributes the alteration to what calls 'the nature

6 Al-Tawḥīdī, *Kitāb al-imtāʿ wa-l-muʾānasa*, p. 116.

of languages and the destiny of meanings'. Another text by the same author, which Laroui does not refer to—extracted from *al-Muqābasāt* —better explains this issue:

> The translation from Greek into Hebrew, from Hebrew into Syriac, and from Syriac into Arabic has betrayed the proper nature of meanings in the concreteness of truths in a way that is not hidden from anyone. If we could perceive the intentions and aims of the ancients in their language, it would be satisfying, judicious and effective, but in every science and in every work there remain insurmountable residues and mysteries which are inaccessible to humankind.

This passage clearly reveals the two interpretations we mentioned earlier to explain the gap that separates meanings when they are transferred from one language to another and from one culture to another.

The first is what we call in our modern terminology the historicist point of view, according to which translation is incapable of transposing the proper nature of meanings because these are forced to emigrate, to be anchored in the historical process and to pass through numerous and diversified mediations. Perhaps to illustrate the impact of this temporal factor, al-Tawḥīdī insists here on the distance travelled by Greek wisdom and the different linguistic stations it crossed to arrive at the Arabic language, which in turn prevented the incarnation of wisdom—'pure and unaltered, and complete with no shortcomings'—in the body of the Arabic language.

This point of view, therefore, assigns the loss of meaning to the plurality of mediations. For if we were able to 'understand the intentions and aims of the ancients in their language' without having to travel all this distance and resort to all these mediations, we would have reached the 'target' and followed the right path without a loss or betrayal of meanings.

However, al-Tawḥīdī seems unsatisfied with this 'historicist' interpretation, as he resorts to another explanation, which concerns us here because it does not attribute the loss of meanings to a historical 'fall', but rather to the nature of meaning itself.

What impedes the attainment of meaning 'proper/as it is' and prevents the achievement of 'specific' meanings, according to this second interpretation, is not mediation and indirectness, but immediacy itself. Meaning here has a self-density that prevents us from discerning its characteristics and clearly delineating its contours.

Mediation, then, is not the cause of loss, since in every science 'remain insurmountable residues and inaccessible mysteries for humankind'. In this sense, Greek wisdom conceals mysteries that even the Greeks themselves were not aware of. Al-Tawḥīdī argues: 'We do not think that all those who lived through the era of the philosophers were able to perceive the aim of the greatest among them and to know the truth of the discourses of their predecessors.' Here, it seems that if mediation has its defects, immediacy has its deficiencies too. The failure to preserve meanings—and al-Tawḥīdī does not say their betrayal—is at the core of meanings, even if they are immediate—and I add here: *especially* if they are immediate.

In this case, the concealment of meaning is not essentially attributable to the errors of the translator, nor to his inability to realize what is in the mind of the author and to know his intentions and aims, but rather to what al-Tawḥīdī calls the residues that are concealed in every science and work. Every science lets something slip through its hands. Any text involves a semiological and semantic density that its author would be unable to fully contain without the escape of 'insurmountable residues'.

There is no way to retrieve the original text, and there is no great difference between 'self-translation' and an ordinary translation. The absence of mediations does not permit the author himself to impose his authority as a privileged translator, to delimit the meanings of the text and determine them, nor to control the receiver, no matter his linguistic and cultural context. It is the sedimentation of residues, which escape any conscious control, that causes the text to escape the authority of its author. It renders meaning uncontrollable, causes it to spread in difference from itself, and ensures that it never appears except in difference and at a distance from itself, especially if it is forced to move between eras and wander between languages.

3
On the Original as Plurality

My friend ceased to translate the French translation of *The Structure of Scientific Revolutions* by Thomas Samuel Kuhn when he realized that an Arabic version based on the original English book had already been published. Of course, he knew that there might be many translations of the same book, but he thought—and probably no one can disagree with him—that a translation based on a mediating language can never reach the level of a direct translation from the original text. He thought that the closer we are to the light of the original, the easier it is for us to understand the texts and assimilate their meanings. Therefore, nothing could measure up to the original.

The book in question broaches issues related to the history of sciences and its ruptures and reversals. My friend knows that the problem of rupture and separation had its heyday in the French context, whether in the history of science or the history of knowledge in general. He also knew that French writers have significantly contributed to the development of this field. But he was aware that the author of the book in English had drawn from them many of his ideas—to the extent that the book in question can be considered an open dialogue with a French tradition known in both the field of the history of sciences and the field of epistemology.

Despite all this, my friend continued to think that the translation of the book would be more faithful if it were done from the original language, and that there was no need to undertake a translation which, in the best case, would be a copy of a copy, a shadow of a shadow.

Nevertheless, my friend was disappointed when he read the translation of the book from its original language. He noticed from the beginning that the translator, who undoubtedly had a mastery of English, was far from grasping the philosophical problematic addressed by the book—especially since this problematic had evolved in the context of the French language. It was evident to my friend that although the translator was closer to the original language, he was far from the philosophical foundations, conceptual terminology and questions raised in that problematic. The translator had dealt with the fundamental concepts of the book, such as reversal, rupture, redesign and revolution, according to an epistemological mentality that was unable to free itself from a linear reading of the sciences and their history. He was faithful to an original, not the original.

My friend now has no recourse but to resume the translation he had given up before, convinced this time that fidelity to one original should not be at the expense of another original, and that the original, though unique, is often originals: we can sacrifice one to save another.

4
Philosophy and Translation

Some never cease to express their astonishment, if not also their disappointment, when our philosophers insist on engaging with Western philosophy, translating its ideas and entering into dialogue with its philosophers. They ceaselessly insist on the need to deal with our own problems, to be interested in our own tradition and to dialogue with our ancestors.

We cannot, of course, underestimate this position, nor deny its goodwill and noble purpose. But we cannot, however, accept it without revealing its principles and the difficulties that prevent its acceptance.

What this position seems to forget is that the invitation to dialogue with our ancestors does not exempt us from the duty to re-examine transference, translation and dialogue with those other than our ancestors. We should not forget that our philosophical tradition is itself a dialogue and a translation.

However, what must be emphasized is that this being the case does not diminish its value as a philosophy—just as our position today on modern philosophy, and our dialogue with it and the 'translation' we give to it, do not strip it of its authenticity. It simply depends on the meaning we give to dialogue and translation, or even to transmission and transfer.

If we understand dialogue as an exchange of opinions on what seems to be evident to the interlocutors; if we postulate that translation is a simple reproduction which does not equal the original, and that it is often inferior to it; if we admit that the transfer of ideas and notions from one culture to another and from one language to another is only a passive imitation, limited to mimicking the other—if we admit all of these premises, it would then be quite natural, perhaps even necessary, to draw the same conclusion reached by the detractors of our philosophers.

But if we consider that transmission and translation are not a mere reproduction of originals; if we assume that writing in another language is always 'another writing'; and if we admit that translation is what permits texts to grow, multiply, survive and even develop—then dialoguing with and 'translating' the other becomes a window to contribute to building universality and grasping meanings which ceaselessly circulate between texts and languages, without the ability of any given culture or language to claim their ownership and exclusive possession.

5

Writing in Another Language Is Another Writing

In this essay, I will try to approach the issue of translation by answering a question which may, at first glance, seem not worth posing: If we are able to read a text in its original language, are we then exempt from reading its translations? Suppose that a French person specializing in ancient philosophy is able to read Aristotle in Greek. Is he then exempt from reading French translations? Suppose that I, an Arab reader, am able to study the texts of Greek philosophy in their original language. Am I then exempt from reading what our ancestors transposed into Arabic? Suppose that I am able to study Descartes's *Discours de la Méthode* in French. Am I then exempt from resorting to the translations of Mahomud Al-khoudhayri, Jamil Saliba and Omar Charni? And suppose that I am able to read Hegel's *Phänomenologie des Geistes* in German. Am I then exempt from examining French versions of the same text?

Some may hesitate to respond to this last example if they had, like me, read that some German scholars rely on the translation of Jean Hyppolite to read Hegel's text. We are here in front of a case which shows that the question is not as easy as it may first appear, that the original may not exempt us from reading translations, just as the translations do not exempt us from reading the originals. This is maybe the reason some editors publish what they call bilingual editions, where they offer the reader, at the same time, the original and its translation, face to face. It is true that there are some who argue that these bilingual publications are unable to justify themselves, for it seems unclear whom they are precisely meant to address. If their reader does not master the language of the original, he will be content with the translation, and if he is able to read the text in its original language, then he will not be in need of any translation.

However, this objection can only be convincing to those who are quick to judge the nature of the relation between the text and its translation—or more accurately, its translations. This relation seems to be one of familiarity or fidelity, despite the infidelity we often say occurs in translation. If translation is bound to this cohabitation with its original 'version', it is because the copy has a passion which does not cease to return to its original and see itself in its mirror. For what characterizes the copy is its constant feeling that it does not pay the original its debt. In this sense, every translation, no matter how valuable it is, always remains problematic. This is maybe why Benjamin insists, in 'The Task of the Translator', that the translation is not exempt from knowing the original. This doesn't mean that it exists without the original, but rather that it cannot exist without it. It doesn't cease to cling to it passionately.[1]

In 'Des Tours de Babel', Derrida dwells at length on the meanings of Walter Benjamin's title for his text, 'Die Aufgabe des Übersetzers' (The Task of the Translator). He affirms: 'The title also says, from its first word, the task (*Aufgabe*), the mission to which one is destined (always by the other): the commitment, the duty, the debt, the responsibility. [. . .] The translator is indebted, he appears to himself as translator in a situation of debt; and his task is to render, to render that which must have been given.'[2] But Derrida hastens to qualify his point by ridding this responsibility of any moral aspect. He affirms that the one in debt in this case is not the translator. The debt does not bind the translator to the author, but a text to another and a language to another. But who is in debt to the other? Or more accurately, what is indebted to the other?

Common sense will retort, without hesitation as usual, and say that children are indebted to their fathers, copies to their models and translations to the original text. But, since the text desires its translation and longs for it, it itself becomes indebted to its translations. For the original, says Derrida, is 'the first debtor, the first petitioner; it begins by lacking and pleading for the translation.'[3]

It is then a desire to exist; as Benjamin says, it is a desire to live, develop and proliferate, and a desire to survive—as if the text grows old in its own

---

1 Benjamin, 'La tâche du traducteur', pp. 244–62.

2 Jacques Derrida, 'Des tours de Babel' (English translation by Joseph P. Graham) in *Difference in Translation* (New York: Cornell University Press, 1985), pp. 175–76.

3 Derrida, 'Des tours de Babel' (English translation), p. 184; 'Des tours de Babel' (French edition), p. 213.

language and longs to travel, migrate and be written again, to don the clothes of another language. Derrida points out:

> [O]ne could then say that each language is as if atrophied in its isolation, meagre, arrested in its growth, sickly. Owing to translation, in other words to this linguistic supplementarity by which one language gives to another what it lacks, and gives it harmoniously, this crossing of languages assures the growth of languages, even that 'holy growth of language' 'unto the messianic end of history'.[4]

In this passage, Derrida has only explained Benjamin's point of view. The latter affirms that any work 'reflects the great longing for linguistic complementation. A real translation is transparent; it does not cover the original, does not block its light.'[5] It calls for it and longs for it at every moment. However, it is the translation that permits the text to survive and develop—but this development could not be what it is if it were not also a renewal and an improvement.

Derrida wrote a letter to explain to his Japanese friend the difficulties in transferring the term *deconstruction* to another language:

> I do not believe that translation is a secondary and derivative act with regard to an original language or text. And as I have just said, 'deconstruction' is a term which is essentially replaceable in a chain of substitutions. This can also be realized between one language and another. The chance of a 'deconstruction' would be that another word (the same and an other) is found and invented in Japanese to say the same thing (the same and an other), to talk about deconstruction and to use it elsewhere—write it and transcribe it, using a word which will also be more beautiful. When I speak of this writing of the other, which might be more beautiful, I obviously understand translation as involving the same risk and opportunity as the poem.[6]

Derrida insists here on the distinction between the original and the translation, on the one hand, and between the principal and the secondary, on the

4 Derrida, 'Des tours de Babel' (English translation), p. 202

5 Benjamin, 'Task of the Translator', p. 260; 'La tâche du traducteur', p. 257.

6 Jacques Derrida, 'Lettre à un ami Japonais' in *Psyché*.

other. The relation between the original and the translation is not a relation of a principal to a secondary, nor even a relation of an offspring to an ancestor. Also, translations are not necessarily a decline or deterioration, where copies move further away from their originals. Translations are an enrichment which carries meaning. They are a risk which can yield unexpected results. Derrida concludes elsewhere: 'The work does not only live a long time by means of its translations, but also longer and better, beyond the means of its author.'[7] Thanks to translations, the text does not merely live for a long time or develop; it lives, survives and even improves.

How do we understand this improvement, this ascension? The issue here is not about, and can never be about, a value-based notion of survival, through which translations become better in quality than their originals, or more superior in literary value and greater in their intellectual depth. For what Derrida intends by the expression *au-dessus des moyens de son auteur* is: beyond his ability. It is the same meaning which Umberto Eco expresses while discussing his experience with his translated texts: 'I used to feel that the text, in its contact with another language, exhibits interpretative potentials which had remained hidden to me, and how translation may sometimes ameliorate this.'[8]

Perhaps the most important thing in Eco's admission is his observation about the interpretative potentials which the text encompasses and which remain hidden to its author, buried in its language. These potentials do not reveal themselves except in another language, and do not appear except when they are written anew. This is perhaps the same meaning Derrida expresses when he says that the text 'lives beyond the means of its author' when it is translated into other languages. Beyond his means signifies: beyond his control and his authority as an author, and the author is rendered inadequate in relation to his text. For in every translation, the author quickly discovers that he is unable to exert his authority over the text, to determine its meanings and control them, to influence the reader regardless of the reader's linguistic and cultural sources. Translation leaves residues which escape any conscious control, and it causes meanings to be in opposition to themselves. These

7 Derrida, *Psyché*, p. 214.

8 Eco, *Dire presque la même chose*, p. 14.

meanings do not attend except at a distance from themselves, and in difference from themselves, especially when they are forced to shift between eras and wander between languages.

In this sense, translation does not only guarantee the survival of the text, that is, its development and proliferation, but it also guarantees the survival of meanings and ideas. In his introduction to one of the French translations of his books, Heidegger wrote: Through translation, the work of thought is transposed in the spirit of another language and thus undergoes an inevitable transformation, but this transformation can become fertile because it brings out into a new light the fundamental position of the question.[9] It is as if the German philosopher, who wrote this introduction in 1932, is here predicting what his thought will become in its French translations. I say translations because Heidegger's texts never cease to be translated and retranslated.

But who would willingly agree to retranslate? It would certainly be someone who studied the original, knew its translations and realized that 'the question can be raised in a new light', and that the translated text conceals 'interpretative potentials' which were hidden from the previous translators as well as from the author himself. For without knowing the translations—and even the original—there would be no retranslation.

We see then that if translations cling to their originals and cannot live without them, it's because the original is itself in urgent need of them. This reciprocal relation, this reciprocal need, obliges us, willy-nilly, to return to the original when we are reading translations, and to go to translations when we are reading the text. It is as if meanings were caught in a movement of translation, and in a game of differences between texts and languages. This is perhaps what makes the return to translations—and the reading of the text in languages other than its own—surpass reading it in its original.

In this way, bilingual editions seem to be neither a publication of the text nor of its translation, but rather a publication of an infinite transition between an 'original' and its copies. This type of writing does not address a reader who hasn't mastered the language of the original, nor one who is entirely unfamiliar with it. Rather, it presumes a reader who is at least able to use two languages and to read the text between the two—a reader who does not concern them-

---

9 Heidegger, *Questions I et II*, p. 10.

selves with the degree of equivalence between the copy and the original, but instead is interested in amplifying the difference between what seems to be identical; a reader who is not inclined to create kinship, but rather to consecrate strangeness; a reader who makes an effort to discover a third text through marrying the two texts and the two languages.

Perhaps this passion for raising questions and creating such a gap is what led all those we have discussed—including Benjamin—not merely to affirm that the copy does not dispense with the original, but that the original itself does not dispense with its translations. They are not content to emphasize that every writing in another language longs for the first writing, but also that every writing is renewed in its strangeness and by its strangeness. Every writing in another language is a re-writing—it is another writing. In this sense, Umberto Eco wrote: 'When I read a translation by a major poet of a poem by another major poet, it's because I know the original and I want to know what it became in the hands of the poet-translator.'[10] Or, to put it in Derrida's terms: because I know the original and I want to see how it evolved.

10 Eco, *Dire presque la même chose*, p. 14.

6
Suspended Translations

Among the presentations delivered at the Conference on Translation and Cultural Interaction, organized by the High Council of Culture in Cairo, I was particularly drawn to the one by Professor Abdelghaffar Makkawi, entitled 'Case Study Report', in which he attempted to depict his experience as a translator. This presentation involved, among other things, an important point that made it not just a case study report, but rather a diagnosis of a phenomenon. Abdelghaffar Makkawi spoke of this phenomenon with sadness, admitting that all the translations he had conducted, despite their diversity, 'were born dead'. Perhaps he was referring to the excellent Arabic translations being published nowadays that seem to have no effect, elicit no reaction and provoke no critique. They are neither exploited nor used. They are not integrated into new intellectual networks, nor engaged in other relations. In brief, they receive no response in the field of cultural exchange.

There are many important translations of major books that confirm what Professor Makkawi pointed out. Let us be content with referring to some of Freud's works translated by Mustapha Safouan or Sami Ali, and those of Locke and Rousseau, without forgetting other significant books such as the *Treatise* by Spinoza, the *Tractatus* by Wittgenstein, and *The Archaeology of Knowledge* by Michel Foucault.

What one might fault Abdelghaffar Makkawi for is presenting the problem as if it concerns him alone, while the issue seems to point to an agent that transcends individuals and practitioners of translation. For the true subject acting in the process of translating is language itself. If Arabic translations are born dead today, it may be because Modern Standard Arabic has not yet been intellectually elevated to the level of the major texts it seeks to transpose. For even if it transposes these texts, it does not truly translate them—and even if it could 'think' within them, it does not transform them into an instrument of thought.

We know that the proliferation of translation is not always the outcome of a favourable reaction to an intellectual call. Some translations emerge from institutional decisions, while others are prompted by cultural events, such as the death of an author or the receipt of an award. Nonetheless, it is rare in the Arab world for translation to occur as a genuine response to a call of thought.

The time when translations of major texts were conducted within a global cultural context has already passed. When Mahmoud Al-khoudhayri launched his translation of *Discourse on the Method* into the field of cultural exchange, Descartes was active not only in Arabic philosophy but also in methods of thought and literary studies. Descartes was already 'acting' across the entire field of thought. Translation at that time was part of a whole, part of a global movement. It was born alive; it even engendered life. It is not surprising, then, that second and even third translations of the same book appeared. But when translation is found orphaned and estranged—that is, outside of the general context—it is only natural for it to be stillborn, or at least suspended, awaiting an intellectual milieu that will adopt it, exploit it, invest in it, oppose it, correct it and perhaps produce a new version of it.

7
Isn't Translation Itself Creativity?

Radwan Ziyyada made an important intervention in recent years with several ambitious translation projects, such as 'The Pioneering Project launched in Egypt by the High Council of Culture, which later became the National Centre of Translation; the Project of the Arab Organization for Translation in Beirut; the Project of the Al-Babtain Foundation (in collaboration with Dar Al-Saqi Books in London); and finally, the project sponsored by Mohammed Ibn Rachid Almaktoum in Dubai.'[1] Despite their importance and anticipated outcomes, these projects direly need further reflection—not only to assess the work they do and the translations they accomplish, but also to consider their agency in the broader cultural sphere.

The writer does not deny the importance of these projects, on which he pins a lot of hope. For him, these projects are 'a reaction to the decline of culture and knowledge in the Arab world through an initiative which aims to translate the maximum of Western knowledge and to transpose it to Arabic culture.' However, he maintains a certain unease about these institutions.

Some may understand this as the apprehension and scepticism we often see in our intellectuals about what may be called 'the institutionalization' of culture. One person has already expressed this scepticism by arguing that: 'The best service that some ministries of culture in the Arab world offer to culture is that they are not concerned with it, thus leaving the affairs of culture to the intellectuals themselves.' However, Radwan Ziyyada's fear is not essentially justified by the existence of these institutions, but rather by translation itself and the obstructive effects its proliferation might have on creativity.

For it does not seem that the writer sees translation itself as a form of creativity. Ziyyada even goes so far as to say that excessive interest in translation may hinder the act of thinking, because translation 'stimulates the skills of the intellectual in translating, but it tends, on the other hand, to neutralize and annihilate his capacities of scientific and intellectual innovation.'

1 *Al-Hayat* (10 April 2008).

Translation makes the elite forget its role in original creativity and keeps it 'dependent on what others write and prevents us from building our own intellectual capacities'.

To respond to these judgments, it may not be enough merely to recall that some of the greatest contemporary thinkers in literature are translators, and that they do not separate intellectual innovation and literary creativity from translation. We should also go further and insist on the effects of translation not only on translated texts, but also on thought and, in particular, on language.

If we understand translation's transformative capacity—if we admit, with many contemporary thinkers, that translation in its essence is a transformation and is what guarantees the life of texts and constructs their history—that is, what guarantees their survival, their development, and their proliferation—and if we admit all this, then the act of translating itself becomes an act of creativity. It is not merely the preparation of raw material for the work of thought. In this way, the translator becomes an author, just as the contemporary author is necessarily a translator.

Still, we must understand Radwan Ziyyada's apprehension of the institutionalization of translation. The response given by those to whom this fear is expressed is that translation has always been under the aegis of an institution in the Arab Islamic world, and they justify this argument with the example of the project of Bayt al-Ḥikma, which was launched by the caliph al-Ma'mun.

It is sufficient to respond to this view by pointing out that the spaces in which translation was practised in European history were also the spaces where the innovation of knowledge was accomplished, and that neither this innovation nor those spaces required an institution to sponsor them.

What we have noticed since the emergence of translation institutions is that they flood the commercial markets with large volumes that are not yet required by the intellectual market, and that many of the translated books are neither read nor used, nor even criticized, as Professor Abdelghaffar Makkawi has already pointed out. This pushes us to share the author's apprehensions, but we will not go as far as he did and fear translation itself. To prove this, it is sufficient to recall the success of some major translations, such as those of Hölderlin.

8

Translation and Philosophy in the Arab World

In what follows, I would like to briefly reflect on this intense and hopeful translation movement currently witnessed by certain institutions and Houses of Wisdom (Buyūt al-Ḥikma).[1] A number of Arab countries are competing to offer major philosophical works in Arabic for those interested in philosophy across the Arab world. It is not necessary, of course, to insist on the importance of this cultural movement, which creates the necessary material conditions without which translation could not take place.

Therefore, there is no need to warn here that we do not intend to diminish the importance of this translation movement. However, this does not exempt us from reflecting on its limits and examining its pros and cons. To translate philosophical texts, it is crucial to foreground the philosophy underpinning this activity and, at the same time, determine the underlying conception of both translation and philosophy.

At the outset, it should be noted that this movement aims to correct the 'mistakes' of a previous era—perhaps viewed by some as an era characterized by the spirit of *bricolage*, a time when translators worked only on the books they had 'at hand', using the languages they knew and the means they had at their disposal. Therefore, the foundational principles of this alternative movement in the field of translation consist in entrusting the task of translation only to specialists, insisting on translation from the original language and prioritizing reference books and foundational texts. It seems that what has been translated so far is a good illustration of the commitment of those overseeing these projects to these principles. To confirm this, it is enough to take a quick look at what the Arab Organization for Translation (AOT) has

1 Translators' note: Bayt al-Ḥikma (House of Wisdom) was a leading public library of the Islamic Golden Age. Initiated by the Abbasid caliph Hārūn al-Rashīd in eighth-century Baghdad, Bayt al-Ḥikma housed a large collection of works translated from the Hellenistic tradition into Arabic. It provided a rich resource in literature, the sciences, architecture, philosophy, and music for students and intellectuals across the Arab world.

achieved in the field of philosophy. This organization has succeeded in making foundational titles available to the Arab reader from the history of philosophy and its various schools and currents.

But does the 'task of the translator' consist merely in offering the reader foundational texts? Let us limit ourselves here to the field of philosophy, since that is our focus: does the translator's task consist in furnishing reference books to those working in philosophy? Can the translation of philosophical works be conducted independently of a gestation of thought?

We have just mentioned the earlier translation attempts. Whatever the defects of those translations, we cannot deny that they were carried out within a broader philosophical gestation. Neither the choice of texts nor the choice of concepts occurred independently of a general intellectual dialectic. In brief, translation did not occur outside of philosophical preoccupation.

We often translated texts that were themselves translated from other languages. We used intermediary languages, as they were referred to at the time. However, those Arabic translations were not separated from a philosophical gestation—or at least from an intellectual preoccupation. Despite their weaknesses, these translations accompanied a broader intellectual debate. We translated some texts by Descartes, but these translations emerged within a cultural context that extended beyond the field of philosophy and into literature and literary methodology. We translated some texts by Marx and Freud from French and English, but we debated at length and hesitated for a long time over certain words and the translation of certain concepts and notions. As an example of our hesitation, let us mention terms such as 'surpassing', 'reification', 'alienation' and 'false consciousness' (for certain texts of Hegel and Marx), and 'repression', 'impulse', 'regression' and 'denial' (for some texts of Freud). We do not observe these debates today among those who translate Hegel, Husserl or Heidegger. Let us be more precise and say that the translation of these philosophers into Arabic is not occurring within a context of intellectual investment in their works.

This cannot be explained solely by the increasingly institutionalized nature of translation in the Arab world, but also by the very conception of translation implied in this activity. For translation here is carried out independently of true intellectual gestation; it is viewed as a kind of adaptation of major texts to make them accessible to Arab readers who want to engage with philosophy and reflect on its tradition. Translation here is seen as a preliminary act. Like the editing of a manuscript, it seeks to make the text ready for anyone who wishes to reflect on it. It also aims to place foundational texts 'in the hands' of the Arab reader. Translation, therefore, becomes a moment that precedes the act of philosophizing. Its aim is to provide the text in Arabic—even if that text must wait 'in the waiting room' until the moment arrives when it will be exploited, used and become the subject of meditation.

But what if half the act of philosophizing resides in the act of translation itself? If philosophy is a dialogue, it is above all a dialogue between texts and languages. In this sense, we cannot separate two moments: the moment of preparing and translating the text, and the moment of using it and reflecting on it. If the majority of contemporary philosophers are translators, it is not because they seek to make texts available, but because they are aware that translating and retranslating philosophical texts is part of the practice of philosophy. I do not mean only that each one of these philosophers—Heidegger, Foucault, Althusser, Lacan, Derrida, Beaufret, Ricoeur—is associated with a book he transposed into his own language, but also that every one of them did not cease to modify the translations of the texts they used. Each of them revised the translation of a text while rereading it—or rather, they reread and retranslated it.

The institutions in charge of translation assumed that the question of philosophy in the Arab world boils down to the absence of major texts, and that the best solution to this problem is to translate these texts into Arabic from their original languages. However, translating foundational philosophical texts is not just about preparing them to become objects of reflection. Translation is neither the editing of manuscripts nor merely the proposition of terminology; on the contrary, it is a thought process, a reinterpretation, and thus a retranslation.

The question of the translation of philosophical texts is not limited to the small number of foundational texts translated into Arabic, but also includes what one of our great translators expressed when he complained that 'his translations were born dead'. Some Arab translators have already translated essential texts in the field of philosophy from their native tongues, but these translations stimulated no reaction in the field of cultural exchange because they were not integrated into new intellectual networks or other relations. They provoked no criticism, and they have not been exploited or used. The confirming examples are numerous. It is enough to mention the translations of some works by Freud by Moustapha Safouan, Zay'ūr and Sami Ali, or the translations of Locke and Rousseau, as well as other important works such as Spinoza's *Treatise*, Wittgenstein's *Tractatus*, or Foucault's *The Archaeology of Knowledge*. These translations are no longer easily found today because their publishers do not consider them worthy of republication.

In this sense, the translation of philosophical texts can only take the form of the practice of philosophy itself. Translation is not simply an act performed on these texts, but an interaction with them. It is no longer a reflection on these texts, but rather a reflection with them. Perhaps this is what explains why philosophical translation remains an infinite act, even within a single language. As long as a philosophical text is a subject of reflection, it will continue to be translated and retranslated. In this case, it suffices to recall our familiar example: the translation of German texts into French.

This has two consequences. First, translation is not just a matter of institutions. The translation of fundamental books cannot be only the domain of organizations, ministries, or Buyūt al-Ḥikma (Houses of Wisdom), collecting major texts to line library shelves. Buyūt al-ḥikma are, above all, a daily practice for anyone who works on and is preoccupied with philosophy. The translation of philosophy, like philosophy itself, is an intellectual concern and a labour undertaken by those who 'till' texts, love language and care for its clarity. While the translation of philosophy may not be able to materially proceed without institutions and organizations, it certainly cannot take place outside the 'laboratories' of thought, nor away from classrooms and spaces of philosophical 'production'.

The second consequence goes beyond the issue of translation and reaches the question of philosophy itself and the mode of its practice in the Arab world. As long as our relationship with major texts does not exceed the level of intellectual curiosity, we will continue to imagine that we can possess these texts simply by translating them into our language, without making a constant effort to distance ourselves from them and to kindle the tension between ourselves and them.

9
Is Translation Always an Instrument of Dialogue? The Case of the Translation of Descartes's Text into Arabic

When I consider the names of philosophers who have been translated from French into Arabic, three names come spontaneously to my mind: Descartes, Bergson and Sartre. Translators have been most drawn to these same names, and only later did they turn to the translation of philosophers who are closer to us in time, such as Bachelard, Althusser, Lévi-Strauss, Foucault and Derrida.

It is true that the interest in Bergson didn't last very long, but we shouldn't forget that most of his important books were translated into Arabic: *Time and Free Will: An Essay on the Immediate Data of Consciousness*, *Matter and Memory*, *The Two Sources of Morality and Religion* and *Creative Evolution*. The latter even received more than one translation. Yet despite the quantitative and qualitative extent of Bergson's translation into Arabic, the presence of the philosopher of duration didn't last long in Arabic, and his translated books did not require re-publication.

The case of Sartre, as we know, is special. No one can deny his strong presence, if not in our schools and universities, then at least in our journals and forums. But Sartre was introduced to the Arab world more as a man of literature, with a new theory of literature and its function, than as a philosopher. To understand Sartre's presence in the Arab world, it suffices to read what the translator of *Being and Nothingness*, Abderrahmane Badawi, wrote in his memoirs:

> Before 1945, I didn't know Sartre had anything to do with existentialism. Before that, I read his first book on psychology, *Imagination*. His last book on existentialism is *Being and Nothingness*. When I read it, I found it far from Heidegger's existentialism and largely a mix of psychological analyses. Since then, I've had little appreciation for Sartre as a philosopher and have considered him mainly a man of letters.[1]

1 Abderrahmane Badawi, *Sīirat Hayātī* (Beirut: Arab Institute for Research & Publishing, 2000).

We can add to what Badawi says here that Sartre was not present in Arabic culture through his texts, but rather as an intellectual—a model of the committed intellectual.

For all these reasons, I want to limit myself here to the one considered the father of modern philosophy. My choice is based on three points: First, Descartes's text is one of the first philosophical texts translated into Arabic; second, the majority of Descartes's works were translated and retranslated into Arabic; and third, the spirit of Descartes has penetrated our schools and universities, and has even been adapted as a method in our philosophical and literary studies. However, I choose Descartes not only for these reasons, but also—and perhaps most importantly—because when we examine the way we select and treat his texts, it becomes possible to respond to a fundamental question: Is translation always an instrument of dialogue? To answer this, we must begin with some historical data.

Descartes's first book to be translated into Arabic, as we know, was the *Discourse on the Method* by Mahmoud Al-khoudhayri, on the recommendation of Cheikh Mustapha ʿAbd ar-Raziq. In the introduction to his translation, published in 1930, the translator gives two reasons that led him to carry out the translation into Arabic. The first reason is general, and consists in 'the great concern in Egypt and the East to know Western culture and the desire of their savants to share with nations which have surpassed them the civilization and knowledge that were behind their progress.' The second reason is that while *Discourse on the Method* was not merely a prelude to all the developments of seventeenth- and eighteenth-century philosophy, it is, for some, the foundation of modern civilization—because, in their view, it is the origin of the French Revolution. As Emile Boutroux observes: 'The renewal of society in 1789 took place in the name of the principle of Cartesian certainty.'

Discourse on the Method would later undergo several retranslations. The first of these was by Jamil Saliba, published in Beirut and sponsored by UNESCO in 1953 under the title *Maqāla fī al-ṭarīqa*.

Meditations on First Philosophy was the second text translated into Arabic. It was translated by Othmane Amine in 1951, again on the recommendation of Cheikh Mustapha ʿAbd ar-Raziq . However, the philosopher of the interior, Othmane Amine, did not justify his translation by referring to modern civilization, as Al-khoudhayri had done. Rather, he viewed *Meditations on First Philosophy* as 'the book of the era, because it encourages thinkers in this materialistic and tumultuous time to consider the concerns of the soul, to reflect, and to engage in an examination of conscience.' This text, too, would later be retranslated in Beirut by Kamel El-Haj in 1971.

The Principles of Philosophy is the third book by Descartes, translated by Othmane Amine in 1962. We shouldn't omit here the translation of some extracts carried out by Najib Baladi in 1959 in the book he devoted to Descartes. It goes without saying that other translations would later appear, such as *Passions of the Soul*. Additionally, Omar Charni's later retranslation of *Discourse on the Method* first appeared in Tunisia and was then reissued by the Arab Organization for Translation in 2008 under the title *Ḥadīth al-ṭarīqa*. Next, extracts appear here and there, either in response to educational and scholarly needs or according to the interest shown in a contemporary philosopher such as Hegel, Heidegger, Bachelard or Foucault, whose philosophy constitutes a dialogue with the founder of philosophical modernity.

In this set of translations, which roughly spans a century, we may distinguish between three approaches to dealing with Descartes's texts. In the first approach, despite the translator's intentions, the text of Descartes in Arabic brings the self back to itself, rather than opening it up to the other. In the second approach, some translators seek, in a spirit of benevolent openness, to define the methodological novelty of the father of modern philosophy. In the third approach, there is an attempt to open up to Descartes's text, not to adopt and use it, but to exceed and separate from it.

We note at the outset that Descartes brings translators and those interested in his texts back to Arabic Islamic philosophy, rather than opening them up to the other or referring them to the history of philosophy in general—and to the history of European philosophy in particular. In 1924, in his book *Al-Akhlāq ʿinda al-Ghazālī* (Ethics in Al-Ghazali), Zaki Moubarak compared the scepticism of Descartes and the scepticism of Al-Ghazali, discovering that the latter 'was the cause for philosophy's stagnation in the East, while that of Descartes led to the progress of philosophy in the West.'[2] In 1967, Mohamed Charif revealed in his book *al-Fikr al-Islami: Manabiʿuhu*

---

2 Zaki Moubarak, *Al-Akhlāq ʿinda al-Ghazālī* (Cairo: Hindawi Foundation, 1924).

wa-Atharuhu (Islamic Thought: Its Sources and Legacy) the influence of Al-Ghazali on Descartes—and even on all of modern philosophy. Similarly, Amine compared the 'Ipseity of Ibn Sīnā' and the 'Cogito of Descartes'. Ibrahim Bayoumi Madhkour showed in his book *Al-falsafa al-islāmiyya* (Islamic Philosophy) that the question of the relationship between soul and body in Descartes has its origin in Ibn Sīnā. This return to Ibn Sīnā through and thanks to Descartes is also noted by Mahmoud Kacem in *Dirāsāt fī al-falsafa al-islāmiyya* (Studies in Islamic Philosophy), by Jamil Saliba in his book *Min Aflāṭūn ilā Ibn Sīnā* (From Plato to Ibn Sīnā), and by Souleymane Dounya in the introduction to his critical edition of *Al-Ishārāt wa-l-tanbīhāt* (The Book of Directives and Remarks).

Hence, Descartes's text—its translation and circulation—did not constitute an opportunity to open to the other and dialogue with it, but rather an opportunity to return to the self and re-examine it, in order to: (1) confirm the Arab's historical precedence; (2) follow the influence Islamic philosophers had on Descartes; and (3) most importantly, bestow cultural legitimacy on Arabic and Islamic thinkers. As if the intention of the translation was not what Al-khoudhayri outlined in his introduction to *Discourse on the Method*, but instead to revive Arabic Islamic thought. The intention was not to infuse new blood into this thought, but to prove that what Descartes says is what we had already said and/or that what he said was due to us. It is as if the value of the Arabic text needed a translation to appear, and this value could only be derived by placing an Arabic text in relation to a European one. In this sense, we later return to *Ḥayy ibn Yaqẓān* by Ibn Tufail through *Robinson Crusoe*, to *The Epistle of Forgiveness* by Al-Ma'arri through *The Divine Comedy*, to *al-Luzūmiyyāt* (The Self-Imposed Compulsion) by Al-Ma'arri through Schopenhauer, to *Dalā'il al-I'jāz* by Jurjānī through Saussure, to *Tahāfut al-falāsifa* by Ghazālī through David Hume, and to the *Muqaddima* (Prolegomena) of Ibn Khaldūn through Auguste Comte.

Fortunately, there is another type of translation—as well as a different choice of texts and commentary—which we find this time mainly in Najib Baladi, in his aforementioned book, where he remarked on the importance of *The Rules for the Direction of the Mind*, and also in some letters Descartes addressed to Mersenne. It is here that the perception of translation and the motivations behind the interest in it begin to shift. The value of Descartes's text is now registered in the history of philosophy, and Descartes is considered a founder of rationalism and the initiator of a new method of thinking, one that provides the emergent field of physics with the philosophical concepts it needs. This methodological significance is what Taha Hussein pointed to when he called us to 'forget our nationalist sentiments and their specificities, to forget our religious passions and everything related to them, and to strictly conform to the real methods of scientific research—for if we do not forget these passions, we will be biased, prone to satisfy our emotions, and obliged to cancel our minds.'[3]

A third approach to the translation of Descartes into Arabic would later appear. For it, Descartes's text represents neither an opportunity to return to the self, nor a methodological model or a lesson in rationality, but rather one of the foundational moments in the history of philosophy and a position on knowledge, science and being—a position that should be surpassed. But this can only be achieved through dialogue and appropriation. This, of course, is realized by the contemporary philosophical 'thrust' that appeared in different areas of knowledge: in epistemology by Bachelard, in anthropology by Lévi-Strauss and in philosophy by Nietzsche and Heidegger.

Each of them would work from his own 'domain' to establish a different dialogue with Descartes's text, which, when translated into Arabic, does not push us to return to ourselves, nor to be content with merely taking inspiration from it in our research methods and modes of thinking. Rather, this dialogue leads us to undermine the foundations of his philosophy and to be convinced that 'we are not where we think, but where we do not think.' It also leads us to understand that knowledge is not only a methodological question, but also an ethical and political issue. The question of knowledge does not consist in searching for the discourse of truth, defining how it can be reached, and the rules governing it. It consists rather in examining the effects of truth generated by discourses. For truth does not depend only on the order of reasons, as the father of modern philosophy believed, but also on the political economy of knowledge and 'the order of discourse'.

3 Taha Hussein, *Fī alshiʿr aljāhilī, alkitāb alʿawwal* (Cairo: Almaktaba almiṣriya, 1926).

Undoubtedly, I am inclined to consider that the third approach is the one that allows the translation of Descartes to serve as an instrument of dialogue. But why couldn't the same be said of the previous two approaches, particularly the second, which seems to open us up to the thought of the father of modern rationalism? To answer this question, we must reconsider what we usually call dialogue. We therefore have to ask the fundamental question: Is the aim of dialogue to unify thoughts or, at least, to achieve a minimum of consensus? Is the intention of philosophical dialogue to search for points of convergence? Does openness to the history of philosophy seek to gather what is dispersed and to achieve harmony? To answer all this, it may be sufficient to recall what Descartes himself said in his *Rules for the Direction of the Mind* about the disagreement among philosophers and their inability to come to an understanding even among themselves.

Philosophy, as an act of resistance, works against all that consecrates sameness and tradition, and it confirms that every apparent agreement conceals an original misunderstanding. In this sense, the dialogue between philosophical texts does not compel a text to find itself in another, or a culture to recognize itself in another, nor even require that a particular culture be transformed into a model to be followed or an ideal to be imitated. On the contrary, the dialogue aims essentially to reveal that what is presented as a point of convergence between texts, philosophers, and cultures might instead be points of divergence, and that what is considered an agreement may in fact embody a disagreement. Yet this disagreement is not so much between the parties in a dialogue as it is a disagreement of thought with itself; it is a self-disagreement.

In this regard, the dialogue between texts and philosophers does not seem to be a mere exchange between parties aiming to reach a minimum level of compromise. Even if it is necessary to speak of compromise as the end goal of dialogue, this compromise must be framed around questions—around the possibility of opening new paths and horizons of thought—not a compromise around what reassures and satisfies, but around what is not reassuring and what is unsatisfying. For the controversial points on which the parties disagree, and which turn the dialogue, as we say, into a crisis, do not only divide interlocutors. They also separate the self from itself and thought from the pre-thought. In other words, they oppose thought to itself while it tries to separate from its own prejudices.

All this happens as if the distance between interlocutors is reduced whenever they move away not only from each other, but also from themselves. This is exactly what seems to be missing in the first approach to the Cartesian text. This approach does not cease to make of translation an occasion to return to the self, and also uses it to phagocytize the other and attribute it to the self. The interlocutor can only come closer to the other when he gains more distance from himself. It is as if agreement between parties in dialogue occurs only at points of divergence, and that their encounters occur only at points of rupture—points of crisis and of causing crises, where the self reconsiders itself, language reconsiders its significations, and culture re-examines its foundations. These are the points at which the self, language, and culture become 'a shelter to host the stranger'. It is perhaps this that translation seeks to achieve; perhaps this is its 'task'.

10
The Draft-Original

When Borges affirms that the text is considered original only because it is one of several possible drafts which pave the way for a text that will be written in a different language, he doesn't intend to promote the copy text so as to diminish the original text, as if the translated text were the pruned, revised, rectified, pure and clean text, as opposed to the original, which is only a draft waiting to find its purity when embodied in another language.

Perhaps the aim of the Argentine thinker was, on the contrary, to show that translation, by seeing the original as a draft, often approaches any text as a pre-text. Translation in this way becomes a kind of quest for the different drafts which hide behind the writer's original, as if the aim of translation were to find the labour of gestation that precedes the birth of the text. Thus, it revives it anew and gives it another life and another language.

We cannot, of course, understand this, since we still see the draft as a dirty text or just an act of 'scribbling' which precedes the final 'editing' of the text. It is maybe necessary for us to free ourselves from the metaphysics of 'blankness' to give the draft its value and consider it as that which represents the genesis of the text and witnesses its repeated, hesitant beginnings—and to see the draft as the text that hasn't been 'buried' yet between the two sides of a book. The draft is the proof of the vitality and activity of the text, but also its difficulty and its decline. It is what testifies to proliferation and development, but also accounts for deletions, scratchings, and erasure.

When translation considers the original as a draft, it does not diminish it, denigrate it or defile its purity, but rather breathes life into it with all that it conceals of blackness and whiteness, so as not to let it seem like an original that precedes all beginnings. We are here not far from what Gérard Genette suggests when he says that, in the relation between an original and a translation, every text is a transparent leaf, a geological being that is smeared with residues—even if the text itself seeks to be perceived as an origin, to appear pure and clean, as if it had freed itself of all its 'strata' and rid itself of all its impurities.

11
When the Copy Surpasses the Original

In an important essay titled 'The Original and the Translation',[1] my friend Abdou Wazen collected a good deal of examples confirming the existence of Arabic novels whose quality was 'elevated' when translated into other languages. The readers of these novels started to love the copies more than the originals because 'these novels, when translated into French, English or German, became less riddled with errors and denser and more fluent.'

This phenomenon raises the following question: Is it about the recklessness of the Arabic writer who is indifferent to language rules? Or is it a problem of the act of translation, which can go so far in the betrayal of its originals that the copies become more faithful than their originals?

To understand this question, we may need to leave our Arabic context, so as to avoid posing the issue within a framework that maintains a respect for the originals (*uṣūl*), and we have to inquire: is the phenomenon more general? Does it occur in other texts and other languages?

My example in the field of philosophy is the French translation of Hegel's *Phenomenology of Spirit* by Jean Hyppolite: Germans themselves resort to this translation to read the original because 'the translation is clearer'.

The issue here does not concern language errors committed by the author of the original, nor the transgression of the principles and rules of the originals (*uṣūl*). It rather concerns the act of translation itself, in that it is sometimes capable of creating copies that surpass their originals. Blanchot wrote on the German translation of *Antigone* and *Oedipus* by Hölderlin:

> The translations of *Antigone* and *Oedipus* were nearly his last works at the outbreak of madness. These works are exceptionally studied, restrained, and intentional, conducted with inflexible firmness with the intent not of transposing the Greek text into German, nor of reconveying the German language to its Greek sources, but of

1 *Al-Hayat* (27 March 2006).

> unifying the two powers—the one representing the vicissitudes of the West, the other those of the Orient—in the simplicity of a pure and toral language. The result is almost frightful.[2]

Translation transgresses norms and 'originals and principles' (*uṣūl*) thanks to this extraordinary work.

2 Blanchot, *Friendship*, p. 61; *L'Amitié*, p. 73.

12
On Translating an Untranslatable 'Concept'

While preparing my thesis on the fundamentals of modern philosophical thought, I encountered many concepts which I found difficult to translate into Arabic. Undoubtedly, the texts of Derrida, among others, were the most difficult to translate. Perhaps his most complicated 'concept' to translate is *différance*, which seems impossible to 'translate' within the French language itself. It is known that the author of *Margins of Philosophy* resorted to this scandal-writing to derive the term from the two verbs *différencier* (*al-khilāf*; differentiate) and *différer* (*al-irjāʾ*; defer).

Therefore, *différance* signifies *al-irjāʾ*, which takes into account 'time and power in an operation that requires an economic calculation, a detour and a delay'. This term also signifies *al-khilāf*, which implies 'a gap, distance and spacing'.

To deal with this term, which is difficult to translate even within French, I thought of the Arabic term *mubāyana*, which I believed could signify the two meanings: the meaning of 'deferring and differentiation' and the meaning of 'spacing, distance, gap and delay'.

Still, I haven't felt that I found the right term—not out of humility, but in accordance with Derrida's thought and his conception of translation, or more precisely his conception of 'the untranslatable'. In this regard, Derrida argues that a text lives only because it survives, and it survives only when it is at the same time translatable and untranslatable. Totally translatable, it disappears as a text, as writing and as a body of language. Totally untranslatable, even within what we think of as one language, it quickly dies.

The most important expression here, of course, is the one which this text emphasizes: 'at the same time' (*toujours à la fois, et en 'même' temps*). This expression means that the philosopher of deconstruction does not consider the translatable independently and separately from the untranslatable. He deconstructs the duality (translatable/untranslatable), and he makes the two terms distinct while they simultaneously approach one another. He also disagrees that the untranslatable is just a stumbling block and an obstacle which hinders the translatable. He disagrees with those who say that translation is possible but can encounter pitfalls, difficulties and obstacles which make it difficult and, sometimes, even impossible. From the start, he considers translation as both difficult and impossible, but still necessary. It is an impossibility that should be attempted, an obstacle that should be overcome, a difficulty that should be faced and a prohibition that should be transgressed. What must be translated is exactly what is untranslatable—that is, what manifests refusal, resistance, stubbornness, and strangeness. Therefore, this untranslatable does not cease to be translated.

Derrida sees translation as a conquest and an invasion as well as a constant struggle with this ingrained resistance. Hence, the concept of the 'untranslatable' has significant importance for him because it is implied in the act of translation—not as what cannot be translated, but as what we do not cease to translate, or as what Derrida stated, 'what we do not cease (not to) translate.' Defining the untranslatable as that which does not cease to not be translated makes the act of translation an infinite openness and a perpetual tension. This conception opens translation to the future and makes what is translatable perpetually contingent on the untranslatable and existing in spite of it. Translation then is a continuous creation and a constant movement between the translatable and the untranslatable.[1]

Such a conception of translation does not permit you to feel that you triumphed over the language—defined the meanings, determined the concept. This feeling of unavoidable disappointment with the act of translation took hold of me, too, every time I wanted to use the term *mubāyana*. For I felt that even if this term combined differentiation and deferring, distance, remoteness and delaying, postponement and temporality, it did not, however, refer to the 'conception' of different identity (*même*) which the philosopher of deconstruction also wanted the concept to contain.

1 Translators' note: Benabdelali is making a terminological effort by creating words and phrases that, until recently, didn't have Arabic equivalents. Here, he uses *al-mā-yumkin*, which means 'the possible', and *al-mā-lāyumkin*, which can be rendered as 'the impossible'. This wording has existed in Arabic, but it has not been rendered in this novel way except in philosophy.

In fact, the *différance*, which is a movement of differentiation, introduces difference into the interior of identity (*même*). It is what makes signification impossible, except in the case where every 'present' element is dependent on the other, conserving the trace of the previous element, opening up to the effects of its relation to an upcoming element. Here, time is used to define being—not to limit it or determine it as Hegelians claim, but to make it suspended in a movement of perpetual temporization, as 'it saves itself'. It is not a saving as understood and determined by the Hegelian dialectic in a limited economy, 'but rather sparing in the sense of conservation and deferral'.

Here, the notion of trace according to Levinas appears as a fundamental notion, which classical modes of time could not account for. The trace is not an absence, but it's not a presence either. According to Derrida, the trace 'is a torn, cracked, mobile, and deferred presence'; it is a presence 'whose erasure is its structure'.

It is clear then that though the term *mubāyana* evokes spacing and temporization, it omits the structure of erasure and does not highlight a sense of time that gnaws and cracks identity (*le même*) and permits it to be realized retroactively (*athar raj'ī*).

This expression *athar raj'ī*, proposed by Mohamed Albanki, seems to me today more appropriate because it summarizes what Derrida means by the notion *différance* (*irjā'*). If this expression makes reference to *athar raj'ī* in Arabic (retroactive effect), which is very well known in legal language, it eludes this language in the same way Derrida seeks to evade the language of the institution and *ratio*. According to Mohamed Albanki, *athar raj'ī* (*effet différantiel*) is a problematic expression which refers, at the same time, to the expression *athar raj'ī* (*effet rétroactif*) and differs from it on all levels: phonetic, morphological, visual and semantic. The term *raj'ī* (*différantiel*) is a dialectical word which opens up to the future, while *athar raj'ī* orients itself to the past, and here lies the similarity and difference.

In memory of Mohamed Albanki

13
Addicted Translation

Gilles Deleuze warns us that we make a mistake by defining the alcoholic as someone who does not cease to drink alcohol. The alcoholic is perhaps the opposite of what we normally think, to the extent that he can be considered as someone who does not cease to stop drinking. He is more inclined to cease than to continue drinking. He perseveres to cease drinking and is always on the verge of abstaining and giving up. He doesn't cease to make it the last glass. According to the language of mathematicians, he 'tends towards the limit'. His definition of the end is analytical, not algebraic.

Gilles Deleuze uses a good expression to designate this link with limits and cessation when he says that

> [A]ddicts always drink the glass before the last. What precisely counts for him is not the last glass but rather the one before the last, because it is this one which 'realizes', at once, his cessation and continuity. He fills each glass as if it is the one before the last. Each glass is a tangent to stopping. Each glass is a stop minus one. The addict does not reach the absolute limit, but the one before the last.[1]

In 'The Balcony of Ibn Rushd', Abdelfattah Kilito recounts that one morning he woke up with a refrain in his head—not from music, as it happens sometimes, but a sentence or a fragment of a sentence:

> I then remembered Mallarmé who, in 'The Demon of Analogy', recounts having been obsessed one day with an absurd sentence: 'the penultimate is dead'. The penultimate, the one before the last, the penultimate syllable . . . But what does it mean the penultimate is dead? Mallarmé left his flat and walked along the street of the antique dealers, and suddenly 'in front of the shop of a lutanist selling

1 'B for Boisson [Drink]', second episode of *L'Abécédaire de Gilles Deleuze*, French television documentary produced by Pierre-André Boutang (1988–1989), originally aired on Arte in 1995, featuring Gilles Deleuze in conversation with Claire Parnet.

> old musical instruments', he felt a sort of revelation that, while illuminating an aspect of 'the inexplicable penultimate', thickens its mystery.[2]

Perhaps the reader will be astonished to know that while I was translating a text that I enjoy, I was attentive to this relationship between the alcoholic and the act of stopping, between ceasing and reaching the end, the penultimate and its 'death'. While translating into Arabic, I found myself addicted to reading and rereading, translating and retranslating. I always find myself close to stopping and ceasing to translate, always on the verge of the penultimate translation . . . which does not cease to die. I then asked myself: After all, isn't every translation always a penultimate version?

If it is the case, maybe we can engage translation in a temporality which is determined by what mathematicians call infinitesimal calculus. Maybe we will raise questions of translation far from the time of filiations and the supremacy of the original, away from the time of interruption, far from the time which sees death only in the end, far from the time of metaphysics, so as to place it in a temporality of repetition, which considers every rupture as a link, every interruption as a movement, every death as a renewed life, every end as a second beginning and every copy as a reproduction of an original.

When Borges affirms that the text is considered original only because it is one of the possible drafts which paves the way for a text that will be written in another language, he maybe wants to show that translation considers every text to be always a pre-text. In this way, translation becomes a witness to the repeated beginnings of the original and a sort of quest for the different drafts which hide behind the author's original version. As if the goal of translation is to bring back the gestation of the birth of the text in order to revive it and to offer it another life and another language.

Undoubtedly, this temporality opposes any approach to the questions of translation within an ethics of fidelity and betrayal, since it is based on a principle which always pushes originals and copies, beginnings and ends, towards the extreme limit. In the aforementioned text, Gilles Deleuze cites

---

2 Abdelfattah Kilito, *Min shurfat Ibn Rushd* (Casablanca: Dār Tūbqāl lil-Nashr, 2009), p. 57.

an expression of Charles Péguy: 'It is the last nymphaea which repeats the first. It is the first nymphaea which repeats all the others and the last.'[3]

Thenceforth, the originals become the ones that mimic their copies, the translation becomes a constant suspension, and the betrayal therefore becomes a temporary fidelity, and the fidelity a transient betrayal. Translation becomes an addiction to translation, and every translation becomes the penultimate version.

3 'B for Boisson [Drink]', *L'Abécédaire de Gilles Deleuze*.

14

Translation and the Notion of the Original

From time to time, I ask myself whether the practitioners in the field of translation are annoyed by the curiosity of philosophers who seem to excessively explore translation as a way to raise their own questions and treat their issues. It is true that there are common points which they share, and that these points involve other practitioners from other fields, but still, a general view of philosophy throughout history leads some to believe—not without reason—that philosophers meddle in domains which do not belong to their specialty.

It's not hard to find support for this point of view. Throughout its history, philosophy was not content with its curiosity, but rather claimed the obligation of patronage and motherhood, and pretended that its task was to lay foundations and establish origins. Perhaps this is why it justified for so long its intervention into the sciences and its scientific curiosity. It required a heated debate and a significant period of time to clarify that science had no need of such a foundation. Gaston Bachelard explained this fact so well that it is useless to recall it here, but he did not, however, strip philosophy of its right to open up to the sciences. However, he refused to let this opening be a kind of legitimacy for philosophy and a sort of applied exercise that a philosopher carries out after having tackled the same questions in his own field.

Going back to the relation between philosophy and translation, I don't think that the aim of the philosopher, in his interest in the questions of translation, is to provide a basis for the positions of linguists and literary critics, nor to do away with the contributions their studies could make to this field. In this context, the expression of Gilles Deleuze, 'extending the text', can help us here. According to this expression, philosophy is able to extend study—and let us say, for what interests us here, that the possible intervention of philosophy in the domain of translation consists of making the linguistic, poetic and literary studies extend to the major questions posed by reproduction, and to the notions of the model and icon, repetition and similarity, difference and origin.

We should insist here on the fact that these notions are deeply rooted in the history of metaphysics, and thus they are difficult to determine and deconstruct. Therefore, they should be tracked down or 'apprehended', to use Nietzsche's phrase, on diverse occasions and in various fields, as if their deconstruction cannot be accomplished in one precise field. Perhaps we could find in Jacques Derrida's deconstruction something that corroborates this perspective, for he deals with the same notion first in the field of anthropology, then in the domain of psychoanalysis, or in the history of philosophy, and then again in the field of translation. According to the language of music, it is about variations within the same melody. But if we prefer to use, as Derrida himself did, a term belonging to the lexicon of war and strategy, we say that these are various 'strikes'.

It becomes all the more clear that we are dealing here with the notion of origin. There might be no time to discuss in detail the various 'strikes' which this notion received in the field of epistemology and the philosophy of science—particularly mathematics—or in the domain of psychoanalysis. We also cannot present the decisive moments where the notion of origin has undergone great upheavals. It's sufficient to pause at what can be considered the great 'strike' this notion received from genealogy.

In the preface to *The Genealogy of Morals*, Nietzsche defines his work as if it were a search for 'the origin' of moral prejudices. He distinguishes between two conceptions of the origin: an origin consecrated by metaphysics, with its 'search for ideal significations and undefined ends', and another origin which tends to be an anti-origin—the one that a genealogical history seeks to establish. There is, therefore, an origin that founds and another one which is being founded.

The first origin is 'a first' origin. It is the founding moment par excellence in which characteristics are defined and identity is determined. It is the moment in which things take on their constant state, which precedes all that comes after it. It is the moment in which things 'are accomplished' to determine the foundation of all that will happen. The origin is the shadowless morning light in which things come forth brightly to occur—'before the fall, before the body, before the world, and before the time'. It is the model before the beginning of the process of reproduction. It is the home of the reality of things—that is, what makes these things what they are, what makes the recognition of their identity and reality possible, what 'founds' them and 'founds' their knowledge.

Genealogy stands opposite this notion of origin and relies on history instead of metaphysics. It seeks to show that the essential secret of things is that things do not have an essential secret, and that essences and identities are made up gradually of things which are strange to them. Genealogy shows that what we find at the beginning of things is not the 'truth' of things, not the origin that founds, not the identity that conserves and shields, but rather dissemination and dispersion.

It is inevitable, then, to linger at the beginnings with all their details—not because these beginnings are a necessity, but because they are a contingency; not because they are a reality, a reality of realities, but because they are 'a kind of error which has the advantage of not being able to be refuted, undoubtedly because the long work of history made it unalterable.' These beginnings are not reducible to an original source; rather, they are what keep track of what has happened in its dispersion and scattering—that is to say, what Nietzsche calls in *Human, All Too Human* 'the little unpretentious truths.'

'The search for provenance', said Michel Foucault, 'does not found. It disturbs what we perceive as stable, moves what we think of as static, fragments what we see as unified, and deconstructs what we imagine to be identical.'[1]

After this brief summary of genealogy's approach, I will permit myself—not to apply it to the field of translation, nor to establish the principle which founds what translators themselves think of as the original text—but rather to extend this philosophical text, the preface to *The Genealogy of Morals*, by in turn opening it to a different field. In a sense, I request—as if I came to translation as an inquirer, not as a founding theorist (I do not say to found)—the extension of the philosophical text. I raise the questions: isn't this the confusion which Nietzsche talks about? Isn't this confusion what originals face when they become implicated in the act of translation—transferred from one language to another, from one writer to another, and from one receptor to another?

---

1 Michel Foucault, 'Nietzsche, Freud, Marx' in *Cahiers de Royaumont*, VOL. 4: *Nietzsche* (Paris: Minuit, 1967), pp. 183–200.

In his text 'The Task of the Translator'—which, as we know, was written as the preface to the German translation of Charles Baudelaire's poems—Walter Benjamin affirms that translation displaces the original from its locus and makes it 'express a great desire for a complementarity of languages'. Translation belittles the original, dethrones it, reveals its weakness, and throws it into the movement of history. 'Translations are what constitute the history of the text', that is, what permit its continuity and survival—but also its growth. Translations distance the text from itself, making it leave its original territory—its significant place—to live in its copies and feed on their ink.

There is no harm in invoking Derrida's commentary on this text again. In his remarks on the verb 'survive'—which Benjamin uses in its German equivalent *Überleben*—Derrida writes: 'The work does not only live a long time by means of its translations, but also longer and better, beyond the means of its author.' Thanks to translation, the original text not only remains and lives, grows and develops, but it also lives on—it survives.

In *al-Muqābasāt* Abū Ḥayyān al-Tawḥīdī writes:

> If the Greeks' notions resonate with the soul of the Arabs, which is characterized by oratory skill, deep knowledge, an ability to enchant which defies all competition, and breadth of intelligence, their philosophy would have reached us as pure, without defect, intact, and without deficiency. If we knew the intentions and aims of our ancients in their language, it would be satisfying, judicious, and efficient. But in every science and in every work, there exist insurmountable residues and inaccessible mysteries for men.

In this sense, Greek philosophy conceals mysteries that escaped not only those who translated it, but also the Greeks themselves. Al-Tawḥīdī writes: 'We don't believe that all those who lived with the Greek philosophers were able to decipher the ideas of the best among them, or the sayings of their predecessors.' It is as if distorting meanings was itself part of the meaning—even before these meanings were transferred into another language.

The originals bear within themselves the capacity to exist outside themselves. This is what Borges refers to when he affirms that a text can be an original only because it is one of the possible drafts which pave the way for it to be written in another language. Considering the original as a draft does not devalue it. As we said about the amelioration evoked by Derrida, it is not an amelioration of value; considering the original as one of the possible drafts that prepare the way for a text in another language is not giving more value to the draft at the expense of the original. Translating, from this point of view, is a sort of quest for the different drafts that hide behind the author's own. Translating is permitting the text to recover the gestation that precedes its genesis—before being buried between the covers of a book. Translating is a quest for the origin of the original, or for the origins of the originals—a quest for 'the little unpretentious truths'.

Translation gives an opportunity to a text to reveal its energies and update its potentials. Translating is an attempt to revive the original. It is a chance granted to another writing, to another language, and to another receiver. In this sense, translations are what witness the repeated and hesitant beginnings of the original. The original is not a model threatened by reproduction and then by perversion, nor is it a perfection altered by any fault, or a whiteness stained by blackness. It is, rather, an openness to unexpected possibilities. Translations are what permit all these possibilities. They revive the text and breathe life into it—with all that life entails—so that it does not appear, as metaphysics would wish, a pure, accomplished original that precedes all beginnings: an original which needs no addition or development, no deletion, scratching, confusion, or drafting (*taswīd*).

15
Exposure

My friend has never been able to imagine the effort and pain required by the revision of the translation of one of his works. For a very long time, he refused to participate in this operation—what they call 'proofing the translation'. He does not wish to involve himself in a process he already suspects of bearing the mark of betrayal. Whenever his translator asks for help in revising the translation, he assumes the translator is trying to make him share the responsibility—and the consequences—of the translation. He is almost convinced that when the translator turns to him, it is merely a tactic to give readers the illusion that the translation is perfectly faithful, so that the translator may then avoid any dispute or objection. How could it be otherwise? The translator now has the author's approval—the tangible proof, the one who created the original text, who presumably knows all its secrets, the nuances of its meaning and the mysteries of its composition. The translator can then reply to any critic: 'You don't understand the text better than its author, who approved and authorized this translation.'

My friend has no doubt that this tacit complicity is nothing more than a trick—perhaps even a scam. He notices this every time he himself tries to translate one of his own texts into another language. For immediately, he encounters the difficulties posed by his own writing—and then discovers the uncertainty of its expressions, the ambiguity of its meanings and the plurality of its interpretations. What is strange is that he feels he wouldn't even have noticed these difficulties had he not attempted to transfer the text into another language. As if it were the translating language that illuminates the original text and reveals to the author what the original language conceals.

In such a case, there is no need to rely on the author or seek his 'support', since the act of translation seems to surpass the author, the translator, and even the text itself. This is precisely what my friend discovered this time. While revising the translation, he found himself not only facing the usual challenges—choosing the right words, maintaining the accuracy of expression, ensuring precision of meaning—but also confronting the necessity of revising the original text. To revise the translation, he found himself obliged to revise the original.

He also realized that the original was riddled with redundancies and repetitions, and that it needed—just like its translation—a refinement of language and style. Translation thus exposes the flaws of the original, or at least demonstrates the impossibility of fully reproducing its rhetoric and structure in another language. If the translation persists in imitating the original and strives too hard to be faithful, it risks becoming incoherent and redundant. As if fidelity, in the translating language, can only be achieved through a certain distance from the language of the original, and through betrayal, in one form or another.

As if, in translation, language is not only, as al-Jāḥiẓ wrote, 'attracting the other language, taking from it and opposing it', but also 'exposing it'.

16

The Virtue of Translation

I had the opportunity to attend a conference on translation where doctoral students reported on the progress of their university research. The meeting was a precious occasion—not to listen once again to already reiterated approaches to translation, but rather to apprehend translation in process and at work, to accompany translators while they are interpreting themselves and being interpreted, questioning and hesitating, advancing and retreating. Our meeting was not a lesson on the pedagogy of translation, but rather a lesson on translation as pedagogy.

We noticed that the majority of students, while presenting their work and discussing the progress of their research, were aware that their field of study is surrounded by many risks. They were fully aware of the difficulty of their purpose and the toughness of their task, which requires them to be faithful in an environment where the individual is always close to stumbling and committing the most abominable betrayals. In short, they were not sharing their triumphs and successes in overcoming the difficulties they faced, but were instead showing the various forms of failure that they had tried to resolve.

It was clear that the translator is one who tends to refuse easy solutions and is more inclined towards doubt than towards certitude. It was also clear that translation is a nursery for critical thought, a school for practising and learning the taste of words, understanding the nuances and perceiving the subtle differences that distinguish one word from another and separate one meaning from another.

The conference was an occasion to experience translation in its pedagogical dimension, but it was also an occasion to confirm that translation is an instrument of modernization. Both students and their professors understood that while translation opens the language to its outside, it permits the latter to test itself in light of other languages. Translation subjects language to a test in which it receives a violent thrust from the foreign. This powerful thrust may revive it, transform it, and, accordingly, change its music and enrich its vocabulary with new and unusual words and ideas. Translation in this sense is not essentially familiarity and kinship, but rather a consecration of strangeness.

This exit does not throw the translator into the lap of the foreigner, but makes him a 'Sindbad' living between languages and surviving between cultures. It makes the translator aware of the virtues of travel, migration, and renewal. It also makes of translation—not only an educational exercise and a tool for modernization—an instrument of openness and liberation.

17

The Language of Translation and the Language of the Original

Perhaps we do not need to dwell too much on the nature of the relationship between the language of the original and the language of translation. It would be sufficient, therefore, to recall al-Jāḥiẓ's saying on this topic, which we have all undoubtedly read in *The Book of Animals*: 'Once the translator (*tarjumān*) speaks two languages, we should know that he treats them with prejudice because each of the two languages draws the other towards it, borrows from it, and opposes it.'[1] The word *ḍaym*, as we know, means in Arabic 'injustice' and 'oppression'. We say *istaḍāmahu ḥaqqahu* in the sense of 'depriving someone of his right'. Between the two languages, then, arises a relation of power—a relation of tension. It is a relation of dissension and conflict.

Are these explanations of al-Jāḥiẓ enough to respond to our question? To respond, maybe, we have to remember what we said concerning the author's revision of the translations of his own texts.

We have come to two conclusions:

The first is that fidelity is, to some extent, dependent on the translation's distance from the language of the original, and on its betrayal.

The second, which concerns us here, is that revealing the characteristics of the original wouldn't be possible without translation, and that the relationship between the two languages is not limited to the fact that 'each of these languages attracts the other towards it, takes hold of it and opposes it,' according to al-Jāḥiẓ, but that each also seeks to 'unveil' the other. This shouldn't be understood here as revealing weaknesses and faults, but rather as an exposure and an unveiling (*une mise à nu*).

In what follows, we will try to determine the nature of this unveiling. To do this, it is inevitable that we refer to the relation of power mentioned by al-Jāḥiẓ and, more generally, to the nature of the relationship that links the

1 Al-Jāḥiẓ, *Kitāb al-Ḥayawān*, p. 76.

original to the translation. Hence, it would be useful here to recall what we have already said about Derrida.

'The title also says, from its first word, the task (*Aufgabe*), the mission to which one is destined (always by the other): the commitment, the duty, the debt, the responsibility. [. . .] The translator is indebted, he appears to himself as translator in a situation of debt; and his task is to render, to render that which must have been given.'[2] But Derrida hastens to qualify his point by ridding this responsibility of any moral aspect. He affirms that the one in debt in this case is not the translator. The debt does not bind the translator to the author, but a text to another and a language to another. But who is in debt to the other? Or more accurately, what is indebted to the other?

Perhaps this is what al-Jāḥiẓ intended by the expression 'a language takes hold of another'. Actually, Derrida here only clarifies Benjamin's point of view, that every text 'expresses its great desire for a complementarity of languages'.[3] Translation calls to the text and longs for it at every moment, but it is also what allows the text to survive and grow. However, such growth does not deserve this name if it is not a renewal and a survival.

We have already shown that the issue does not—and never will—concern a promotion of value, by which translations become better in quality, more prestigious in literary value or superior intellectually to their originals. For the significance of Derrida's expression 'beyond the means of its author' is just that: beyond its potential.

Maybe this is what should be understood as what we have called 'unveiling', because we are here facing an act similar to a psychoanalytic reading of a text, which unveils its unconscious and reveals what remains—and must remain—beyond the capacity of the author and the capacity of the translator.

---

2 Derrida, 'Des tours de Babel' (English translation), p. 175–76; 'Des tours de Babel' (French edition), p. 211.

3 Benjamin, 'La tâche du traducteur', p. 257.

18
Translation and Identity

One of the French historians of the theories of translation reports that in the midst of the Napoleonic occupation in 1808, some intellectuals wanted to compose a collection of the best German poems to make them accessible to the public. Of course, the nationalist intention of this project was clear. When the authors of this future project asked Goethe for advice on the choice of poems, the sole piece of advice he gave them was to include also German translations of foreign poems—first, because German poetry, since its origins, had owed most of its forms to the foreign, and then because these translations, according to him, were creations that authentically belonged to the national literature.[1]

During the occupation—a historical period in which national identity is usually codified—Goethe recommended considering foreign texts translated into German as part of German literature. What can we deduce from this?

We should pause at two essential issues. The first concerns the nature of this openness suggested by Goethe. It is clear that the author of the *West-östlicher Divan* is not content merely to emphasize that national literature expands to integrate and include foreign literatures. Let us consider what he meant by *Weltliteratur*. He does not mean, by 'world literature', all past and present literatures that an encyclopedic view would summon, nor does he mean all the major works that have attained universality and become the heritage of civilized humanity.

Die Weltliteratur, on the contrary, is a historical concept that concerns the relationship between different national literatures. The era of 'world literature' is the era in which literatures are not merely content with interaction but realize their existence as part of an ever-increasing interaction.

This concept of *Weltliteratur* implies a theory about the self and the other, about identity and difference—a theory by virtue of which the departure of identity outside itself is consubstantial to it, and its awareness of itself becomes

1 Berman, *L'épreuve de l'étranger*, pp. 94–95.

a changing awareness, contingent on increasing interaction with the other. What concerns us here is that Goethe sees translation as the means of this departure. This is exactly what he intends when he says that translations constitute creations that are not separate from German literature, or when he affirms that translation is a tool for building universality. What concerns him in translation is the fact that it is a tool to modernize language. Goethe uses the term *Auffrischung*, or 'refresh'. Translation is a tool to revive literature and language. Thanks to translation, language breaks from itself and is transplanted elsewhere, away from its original place. When the German language transposes Shakespeare's literature, we should not think, according to Goethe's conception, that Shakespeare will simply speak German, but rather that the German language will be revived in and by Shakespeare.

It is perhaps the same revival that French thought experienced during the second half of the last century when it engaged in translations and retranslations of German literature. Heidegger had already predicted this 'revival' in his 1932 introduction to one of the French translations of his lectures.

Any historian of French philosophy must include these German texts, which were transferred into French, in the history of contemporary French philosophy. The French language revived them while being revitalized by them. For further proof, it is enough to recall the translations of Husserl by Paul Ricœur, of Hegel by Jean Hyppolite, or of Kant by Victor Delbos . . .

According to Blanchot, the translated text mimics the act of creativity. This act works with everyday language—the one in which we live and are immersed—seeking 'to give birth to another language, which looks the same, but which constitutes its absence and its difference—a difference that does not cease to happen and does not cease to hide.'[2] It is then a desire to leave, or what Walter Benjamin expressed as the desire to live, to grow and proliferate—the desire to survive.

To explain the difficulties of transposing the term 'deconstruction' into another language, we can recall here again what Derrida wrote in 'A Letter to His Japanese Friend':

> I do not believe that translation is a secondary and derivative act with regard to an original language or text. And as I have just said,

2 Blanchot, 'Traduit de', pp. 186–87.

> 'deconstruction' is a term which is essentially replaceable in a chain of substitutions. This can also be realized between one language and another. The chance of a 'deconstruction' would be that another word (the same and an other) is found and invented in Japanese to say the same thing (the same and an other), to talk about deconstruction and to use it elsewhere—write it and transcribe it, using a word which will also be more beautiful. When I speak of this writing of the other, which might be more beautiful, I obviously understand translation as an adventure of the poem and its opportunity'.[3]

This also leads us to the second issue raised by Goethe regarding the anthology of German poems. By openness, Goethe does not mean bringing the other to the self and abolishing difference, nor does he mean dissolving the other and diluting it into the self. For we all know that Goethe is one of the most scrupulous thinkers when it comes to preserving difference. The opening of language to its outside does not mean, for him, absorbing and subduing foreign literatures. He says:

> [W]e must not get into an immediate conflict with the foreign language. We must reach the untranslatable and respect it; for therein lies the value and character of every language [. . .]. In translation, we have to reach what is untranslatable, for only in this case do we become conscious of the foreign nation and the foreign language.[4]

Goethe does not mean attracting the other to the self and 'gobbling' him down, but rather going towards him—opening the text, opening the culture to the otherness of the other, and enriching the text and culture by fertilizing them with the other language and by 'hosting the stranger'.

What concerns Goethe in the act of translation is not making foreignness disappear, nor denying the otherness of the other, but rather consecrating foreignness, and making of this act an opportunity for the self to become conscious of itself as it departs, interacts, and separates from itself. As if all that concerns him in the act of translation is this migration that causes the German language to Gallicize, Anglicize and be revitalized.

3 Derrida, 'Lettre à un ami Japonais'.

4 Quoted in Berman, *L'épreuve de l'étranger*, p. 97.

To understand the nature of this departure, we have to compare it to another one—where the self perceives itself only through the perception of the other, a departure that can become conscious of itself only through the other's recognition of it.

It is here that texts acquire their importance, and even their national status, when they are written in a foreign language and later translated into a national language. In this case, translation is not a 'reviviscence', but rather a means of seeking recognition—a bridge between identity and itself.

We have already mentioned, on another occasion, the second type of departure that we experience today in our Arab world: we notice that some of our writers publish their books in a foreign language and then work on the translation into Arabic. We have already noted how Abdallah Laroui observed that if he had not written his book *L'idéologie arabe contemporaine* in a language other than Arabic, it would have been neglected in the Arab world. Perhaps the most important idea Laroui seems to affirm here is that the Arab reader is the one whom the text addresses—even if it is written in a different language. Here, translation becomes the way to reach the intended reader. For the Arab reader to receive the text, it would be better, and even necessary, for it to be translated. It should be transferred to him via another language. It is necessary here for the other to intervene as a mediator between the Arab writer and the Arab reader, as if the Arab intellectual arrives at himself only through another, and speaks his language only through another language. Arabic culture today knows itself not only through the other, but also through the perception that the other has of it. Therefore, it does not experience translation as an editing and publishing activity, but rather as a lifestyle and a mode of existence and being.

We see here that if the first departure was an opening, a fertilization, a transformation and a revitalization, the second one is a submission to the other. While translation subjects language to the violent thrust that ensues from the foreign language, it is here a consecration of the foreignness of the self to itself.

One may retort that this question does not concern Arabic culture alone, or that it is merely one of the residual effects of a phenomenon marking all postcolonial cultures. But it is a phenomenon we still witness today—even in countries that were essential parts of colonization. In fact, French culture itself is beginning to live through translation as a means of confirming its identity. Suffice it to say, many French writers today seek to reach the French reader through English.

Here, we understand the difference between world literature and globalized literature. Globalized literature is determined by relations of power governed by the predominance of a major structure that imposes its themes, styles, and language. In globalized literature, the text acquires its identity only through an other, which is imposed as a model. This does not mean that world literature does not exist in cultures shaped by relations of power. However, there is a wide difference between relations in which the work of difference is able to thrive, and relations subject to standardization, in which any difference is repressed. In this second type of relation, translation becomes a tool for canonizing the dominance of one specific language and a means of annihilating identity. In the first type, by contrast, it revives identity and consecrates difference.

This is perhaps exactly what Umberto Eco means when he says: 'The language of Europe is translation.'[5]

In brief, there are two opposing functions of translation: in one, the interaction between cultures and navigation between languages is subject to power relations, whereby one language occupies the centre of sovereignty and becomes the model and medium through which identity gains legitimacy, culture derives its specificity, and texts acquire their value. The opposite opens one culture onto another, approaches it from a distance, and communicates while remaining separate.

Translation, then, becomes an instrument that allows culture to test itself in relation to the other, and a means by which identity subjects itself to examination under a powerful thrust from the foreign. It is this force that allows identity to feel its own strangeness—not only in encountering the other, but in encountering itself. In this sense, translation becomes a means by which culture separates from itself, language separates from itself, and the ego separates from itself. It is only through this that translation consecrates difference, nourishes culture and revitalizes identity.

---

5 Umberto Eco, 'The Language of Europe Is Translation', lecture presented at the conference of ATLAS Assises de la traduction littéraire in Arles (14 November, 1993).

19
Hosting the Stranger

In the conclusion of his book *Lan tatakallam lughatī* (Thou Shall Not Speak My Language), Abdelfattah Kilito discusses Mattā Ibn Yūnus's translation of Aristotle's *Poetics*. He stops at two words: (*ṭraghūdiyā*) *tragœdia* and (*qūmūdiyā*) *comœdia*, which are rendered as 'panegyric' and 'satire', and he wonders whether Mattā 'had, at that time, a choice to translate these terms otherwise'.

We know that in the same era, in a domain other than literature (*adab*) and poetry, translators faced the same strangeness and the same difficulties. But when they felt that their language was deficient, they created neologisms, coined new concepts, and forced the Arabic language to 'host the stranger' and to go towards the other. They also spoke of *al-kammiyya* (quantity) and *al-kayfiyya* (quality), *al-ʾays* (being) and *al-lays* (non-being), *al-māʾiyya* and *al-māhiyya* (essence). They even allowed, at least at the beginning, 'strange' words to invade their language, using terms such as *ʾusṭuquss*, *kategorias* and *hylé*. This is what Abū Naṣr Al-Fārābī confirms by saying:

> The philosophy that the Arabs possess today was transmitted to them by the Greeks. The translator, in order to find equivalent concepts for this philosophy, followed the same paths we mentioned earlier. Nevertheless, we encounter some who exaggerate in claiming that these concepts should be expressed exclusively in Arabic, which may lead to confusion. For instance, for two concepts they give one equivalent in Arabic: they call *usṭuquss* '*ʿunṣur*', and they also call *hylé* '*ʿunṣur*'—whereas *usṭuquss* should not have *al-mādda* or *al-hylé* as equivalents—and perhaps they use either *hylé* or *ʿunṣur*. But the concepts they kept in Greek are very few.

In this extract from *Kitāb al-Ḥurūf* (The Book of Particles), an appositive sentence indicates how translators set up equivalents to philosophical concepts. What are the ways by which the concepts are transposed into Arabic? Al-Fārābī responds in the same book to this question:

> If philosophy arises, its followers will necessarily have to express ideas previously unknown to them, and thus must proceed in one of the following ways. If philosophy has been transmitted to their nation (nation B) by another nation (nation A), its followers must review the words by which nation A expressed philosophical ideas and distinguish, among the commonly known meanings in the two nations, those that were transmitted to nation A. If philosophers succeed in making this distinction, they should draw from the language of their own nation the words by which it expressed those same common ideas, as such, and make of these words philosophical concepts. They may find that there are ideas in philosophy which nation A designates by names related to common ideas unknown to nation B and for which it therefore has no terms. If these ideas resemble other common ideas known to nation B, for which it has terms, it is preferable that the philosophers abandon the terms of nation A and look for those most analogous among their own common ideas. They must then take the expressions by which they designate these ideas and use them to designate philosophical concepts. [. . .] If there are ideas in philosophy that do not originally correspond to common ideas for nation B—which is quite inconceivable—the philosophers then have three options: either give them new terms from the alphabet of their language, or combine—arbitrarily—these ideas with others to express them, or express these ideas with words borrowed from nation A, after adapting them to make them easy for nation B to pronounce. This concept, then, will be very strange to nation B, since it would previously have had neither it nor anything analogous to it.[1]

What is interesting in Al-Fārābī's text is that he considers 'common names' as an essential source—the unique and shared source from which terms can be derived. No mention is made here of a possible meeting between two cultures, Arabic and Greek, in other cultural fields, such as that which is called *adab* in classical Arabic culture.

1 Al-Fārābī, *Kitāb al-Ḥurūf* (Beirut: Dar El-Mashreq, 1986).

This fate will later place *Poetics* in the hands of a philosopher—not to translate it, this time, into Arabic, but rather to summarize it and comment on it.

In *Lan tatakallam lughatī*, Kilito dwells, like Borges, on the difficulties or the embarrassment Ibn Rushd felt while discussing the *Poetics* of Aristotle. However, we can say that Ibn Rushd was firm with regard to the book of the First Teacher, to the extent that he permitted himself to say:

> All this belongs to them, and we have none of it—either because what was mentioned is not common to most nations, or because, in this matter, the Arabs were seized by something outside nature. This is evident, for he (Aristotle) could not establish in this book what is proper to them, but only what is common to ordinary nations.[2]

Ibn Rushd then discards these difficulties, affirming that what is unusual is Arabic poetry. We can imagine the embarrassing situation in which the Muslim philosopher finds himself when he confirms that 'what was given to the Arabs was not common', but at the same time does not have the linguistic tools to rectify the translation and put things in their proper place.

Perhaps this is what would later lead many researchers to regret this position. There are even some who consider this error of Ibn Rushd a blow to Arabic literature and Arabic culture as a whole. This is what Abderrahmane Badawi expressed in the preface to his translation of the *Poetics*:

> Let us imagine that fate had wanted this book to be understood in its truth, and the subjects, opinions and principles which appeared therein to be adopted. Arabic literature would have thus been concerned with the higher arts of poetry, i.e., tragedy and comedy, since the time of its prosperity in the 3rd century Hijri (AH), and the whole face of Arabic literature would then have been different.[3]

What is reproached to Ibn Rushd here is not a deficiency related to what we call literary translation—for he was not the translator of the book. As we know, it was Mattā Ibn Yūnus who translated it, not from Greek, but from

2 Ibn Rushd, *Kitāb al-Shiʿr* in *Kitāb Arisṭūṭālīs fī fann al-shiʿr* (Abderrahmane Badawi trans.) (Beirut: Dār al-Thaqāfa, 1973), p. 246.

3 Abderrahmane Badawi, 'Muqaddimat fann al-shiʿr' in *Kitāb Arisṭūṭālīs fī fann al-shiʿr*, p. 51.

Syriac—but instead that he did not master what Roman Jakobson calls inter-semiotic translation.

We know that the *Poetics* is about theatre—that is, precisely an art which Arabic literature could not know before the nineteenth century. It was only by chance that an opportunity to transmit theatrical art itself appeared, with all the complexity that an inter-semiotic translation requires, but this time, between two contemporary cultures: Japanese culture and European culture.

We may ask: Why, exactly, this repeated reference to theatre—and particularly to theatre as an untranslatable cultural specificity?

We may find a response to this question in Heidegger's 'A Dialogue on Language between a Japanese and an Inquirer'. It explores the difficulties of translating the Japanese term *Iki* into German so as to make its meaning accessible. The Japanese interlocutor says: 'Certainly, and especially because the foreground world of Japan is altogether European or, if you will. American. The background world of Japan, on the other hand, or better, that world itself, is what you experience in the Nô play.'[4] The Japanese then explains the specificities of this theatre, the most important of which is the empty scene. He concludes: 'To us, emptiness is the loftiest name for what you mean to say with the word "Being".'[5]

We realize how theatre can express a cultural specificity insofar as it develops concepts which are related not only to time and space, but also to being and non-being.

The Japanese speaker begins by admitting to his interlocutor: 'since the encounter with European thinking, there has come to light a certain incapacity in our language.' He then presents the critical situation of Japanese culture, which finds itself obliged to adopt Western metaphysical concepts—with all the apprehension that accompanies this inevitable operation. It is as if Japanese culture is forced to appeal to Western thought in order to supply it with 'the concepts to grasp what is of concern to us as art and poetry'.

Iki is a concept which means 'a sensuous radiance through whose lively delight there breaks the radiance of something suprasensuous'.[6] This transla-

---

4 Martin Heidegger, 'A Dialogue on Language' in *On the Way to Language* (Peter D. Hertz trans.) (New York: Perennial, 1971), p. 17.

5 Heidegger, 'Dialogue on Language', p. 19.

6 Heidegger, 'Dialogue on Language', p. 14.

tion presents the following problem: the link between the binary sensuous and supra-sensuous proceeds from a conception specific to Western aesthetics, and it does not take into account the aim of the Japanese word. In reality, Western aesthetics remains conditioned by the metaphysics which generated it; Western metaphysics remains governed by binaries, such as rational and sensuous.

The dialogue continues between the German and the Japanese. The latter suggests translating *Iki* as 'what can charm with grace' (*ce qui vient charmer avec grâce*). But they quickly discover that this translation corresponds instead to the definition of Western aesthetics, for the memory promptly evokes what Schiller and Kant wrote on the category of 'grace' in its relationship to the aesthetic object.

The dialogue ends with the fear that Western culture will absorb Japanese concepts. This is what pushes Heidegger—either in this text or in others such as *The Speech of Anaximander* and *What Is Called Thinking*?—not to consider translation only as a *propensity* to go towards the other in the radical sense of that expression. Hence, Heidegger insists in *What Is Philosophy*?, for example, on the necessity of listening to Greek words with Greek ears, and of going to the original place. This is what he highlights in *The Speech of Anaximander* when he places the expression 'to translate ourselves' in front of the translated speech—an expression we must hear in its legal sense: I mean that we appear before this speech and submit ourselves to the questions it poses.

Thus, the German and Japanese sayings can communicate and touch each other, and stand at a certain basic proximity to each other, only if they are scrutinized in relation to contexts and traditions that go far back in time—only if they are taken out of their closed contexts, and only if they invite the stranger and appeal to the stranger.

Instead of attracting the other to the self and creating a theory of translation that seeks to abolish cultural and linguistic differences, and attempts to transpose a text from one language to another (without giving the impression that it is translated) in such a way that the translated text speaks the language of the translator, reveals his personality and belongs to his culture; instead of a translation that aims to overcome the distance between the translator and the author, to abolish the difference between the original language and the translating language; instead of a translation that denies itself as translation and seeks to offer up a text 'as if it hasn't been translated'—a text that erases the act of translation, a text in which we do not smell the aroma of the other language, the aroma of the 'foreigner', of strangeness, of otherness, the aroma of the other, the aroma of difference—Instead of this kind of translation, there is another one which aims to open the culture, to open texts to the outside: a translation which is, according to Heidegger, 'a transformation'. However, we should not understand this as a unidirectional transformation. Translation does not only transform the translated text, but also transforms, at the same time, the translating language.

Translation, then, must be problematic. It should not pretend to overcome all difficulties, erase all distances, or abolish all differences. It has no way out but to admit its defeat in front of the untranslatable, in front of what testifies to strangeness, distance, and otherness, and in front of what refuses to be dominated and subdued, annexed and ingested. This means that it has to recognize the other as an other. In this sense, Goethe says:

> [W]e must not get into an immediate conflict with the foreign language. We must reach the untranslatable and respect it; for therein lies the value and character of every language [. . .]. In translation, we have to reach what is untranslatable, for it is only in this case that we become conscious of the foreign nation and the foreign language.[7]

Facing the untranslatable does not simply mean facing linguistic difficulties that emanate from the weakness or incapacity of the translator. It is not the translator who stands impotent before a text, but rather the language itself that stands before another, the culture itself that stands before another. It is not, then, a matter of inability, but rather a recognition of the 'otherness' of the other. Bringing languages closer to each other, as translation tends to do, is at the same time to distance them from each other. While uniting languages, translation creates—by the same act—difference between them and exacerbates the tension of this difference. Translation is not only a creation of familiarity; it is also a consecration of strangeness. It is hosting—but always 'hosting the stranger'.

7 Quoted in Berman, *L'épreuve de l'étranger*, p. 97.

Translators' Afterword

Thinkers who have dealt with the issue of the Arabic Islamic heritage, such as Mohammed Abed al-Jabri (1935–2010), Ali Oumlil (1940–) and Muhammad Al-Mesbahi (1945–), did not pay due attention to the issue of translation, although it played a crucial role in making much of the Greek heritage generally accessible. Benabdelali's writings are more in dialogue with modernist thinkers within the French Arab tradition—Abdelkebir Khatibi (1938–2009) and Abdelfattah Kilito (1945–)—who gave great importance to the issue of translation as well as to the issue of French–Arabic bilingualism.

Very little of Benabdelali's work has been translated into English. His *Writings on Translation* have already found a way to the French reader through Kamal Toumi's 2006 translation. Benabdelali's work is available in English, and readers will now have a sense of how they are in conversation around the subject of translation.

The translation of the two books required about two years due to the complexity of Benabdelali's thought. His Arabic and his prose style combine a clear-eyed but complex philosophical rigor with an invitational mode of address, and to achieve this same effect in English required us to work through numerous drafts—often rewriting specific passages multiple times—hoping to find the right tone, the right word, or the clear expression of a complex idea. Two readers generously agreed to look over early drafts, if only to confirm that our work was moving in the right direction: we wish to thank Sam Wilder, and we especially thank Brahim El Guabli for his attentive, thorough and extremely insightful suggestions and corrections.

To mediate the linguistic and cultural differences between Arabic and English, we resorted to various translation procedures such as word-for-word translation, adaptation, paraphrase, interpretation and footnotes. Word-for-word translation was used whenever we felt the author communicated meaning with a clear, straightforward structure. It was also used to preserve the colour of the original language, giving Benabdelali a chance to speak his mind in English and complicating the boundaries between the two languages.

However, this technique was not possible most of the time due to the wide linguistic gap between the two languages. When meaning was impossible to communicate in a word-for-word rendition, we focused instead on bringing over the meaning of a given idea or sentence. The wide use of figurative language and examples of classical Arabic in Benabdelali's book forced us to work primarily in this manner, but we always attempted to keep the structure as close as possible to the original. Al-Jāḥiẓ's citations, for instance, were not easy to render in English due to their complex terminology and structures, which required us to focus on meaning-only translations or, on some occasions, resort to paraphrase.

It should be noted that we chose to translate Benabdelali's own translations of his cited texts, and hence these citations are often translations of translations. Benabdelali would call this a 'double betrayal', and this is but one way our translation performs the very theories of translation he advocates. Additionally, we often consulted the original citations that the author had translated from French in order to better grasp the right meaning in Arabic. This led us in many instances to add certain words that do not appear in Benabdelali's translation but are helpful in communicating the meaning of the text. The French version offered us a 'second original' to consult in order to compare and clarify our own efforts.

The dense terminology of Arabic required us to use footnotes in the translation of words that do not have equivalents in English or that have more than one meaning in Arabic. Some proper nouns, like 'The House of Wisdom', needed footnotes to convey their historical background and to help the English reader understand their theoretical context in the translation. The author also used words that carry many meanings in English, such as the term *naskh*, which can mean abrogation, copying or reproduction depending on the context. This required us to use parentheses or footnotes to clarify the meaning—or meanings—intended by the author. Last but not least, some word choices in the translation were needed to preserve the precision of the English text without losing the texture of the Arabic original.

The reader will have noticed numerous repetitions throughout the book; sometimes Benabdelali will repeat whole passages, verbatim or with slight variations, in order to begin a new line of thinking or to conclude a new set of ideas; quotations are also repeated and revisited, in part or in whole, for the same purpose: to generate new starting points for thought. We have left these repetitions as they are, rather than editing them out, not only because they illustrate Benabdelali's process, but also because such repetition is very much a hallmark of Arab philosophy and thought.

In truth, the translation of this philosophical text on translation into English was as difficult as the complexity of the Arabic language itself, where grammatical structures and terminology are suffused with the manifold layers of meaning, identity and culture found in the Arab world. We are excited to introduce Benabdelali's writing to new readers and new scholars, and we thank everyone at Seagull Books for bringing this book into the world. Special thanks are owed to Omar Berrada and Emily Apter, who supported this project from the very beginning. And we are infinitely grateful to the Elsewhere Texts series editors Gayatri Chakravorty Spivak and Hosam Aboul-Ela for believing in this work; it belongs nowhere else.

Marouane Zakhir and Christian Hawkey

Bibliography

Al-Hayat, 10 April 2008.

Al-Fārābī. *Kitāb al-Ḥurūf*. Beirut: Dar El-Mashreq, 1986.

Al-Jabri, Mohammed Abed. *Al-ʿAql al-akhlāqī al-ʿArabī*. Casablanca/Beirut: Arabic Cultural Centre, 2001.

Al-Jāḥiẓ. *Kitāb al-Ḥayawān (The Book of Animals)* (Abdessalam Haroun ed.), vol. 1. Beirut, 1969.

Al-Tawḥīdī, Abū Ḥayyān. *Kitāb al-imtāʿ wa-l-muʾānasa* (Ahmed Amin et al. eds). Beirut: Al Maktaba Al Messriyya, 1953.

Badawi, Abderrahmane. *La transmission de la philosophie grecque au monde arabe*. Paris: Vrin, 1968.

Badawi, Abderrahmane. *Sīirat Hayātī*. Beirut: Arab Institute for Research & Publishing, 2000.

Barthes, Roland. *Leçon*. Paris: Éditions du Seuil, 1978.

Barthes, Roland. 'Lecture in Inauguration of the Chair of Literary Semiology, Collège de France, January 7, 1977' (Richard Howard trans.). *October* 8 (Spring 1979).

Benjamin, Walter. 'La tâche du traducteur' in *Œuvres*, vol. 1 (Maurice de Gandillac, Rainer Rochlitz and Pierre Rusch trans.). Paris: Gallimard, 2000.

Benjamin, Walter. 'The Task of the Translator' in *Selected Writings, Volume 1: 1913–1926*. Cambridge, MA: Harvard University Press, 1996.

Berman, Antoine. *L'épreuve de l'étranger*. Paris: Gallimard, 1995.

Blanchot, Maurice. 'Traduire' in *L'amitié*. Paris: Gallimard, 1971.

Blanchot, Maurice. 'Traduit de . . . ' in *La part du feu*, new edn. Paris: Gallimard, 2001.

Blanchot, Maurice. 'Translated From . . . ' in *The Work of Fire* (Charlotte Mandell trans.). Stanford, CA: Stanford University Press, 1995.

Blanchot, Maurice. 'Translating' in *Friendship* (Elizabeth Rottenberg trans.). Stanford, CA: Stanford University Press, 1997.

Blanchot, Maurice. *The Infinite Conversation* (Susan Hanson trans.). Minneapolis, MN: University of Minnesota Press, 1993.

Blanchot, Maurice. *L'Entretien infini*. Paris: Gallimard, 1969.

Borges, Jorge Luis. *Enquetes 1937–1952*. Paris: Gallimard, 1957.

Deleuze, Gilles. 'Simulacre et philosophie antique' in *Logique du sens*. Paris: Minuit, 1969.

Deleuze, Gilles. 'The Simulacrum and Ancient Philosophy' in *The Logic of Sense*

(Constantin V. Boundas ed., Mark Lester and Charles Stivale trans.). New York: Columbia University Press, 1990.

DERRIDA, Jacques. 'Des tours de Babel' (1980) in *Psyché: Inventions de l'autre*. Paris: Galilée, 1987.

DERRIDA, Jacques. 'Des tours de Babel' (Joseph P. Graham trans.) in *Difference in Translation*. New York: Cornell University Press, 1985.

DERRIDA, Jacques. *La Dissémination*. Paris: Éditions du Seuil, 1972.

DERRIDA, Jacques. 'Lettre à un ami Japonais' in *Psyché: Inventions de l'autre*. Paris: Galilée, 1987.

DERRIDA, Jacques. *Parages*. Paris: Galilée, 1986.

DERRIDA, Jacques. 'Plato's Pharmacy' in *Dissemination* (Barbara Johnson trans.). London: Athlone, 1981.

DERRIDA, Jacques. 'Sémiologie et grammatologie' in *Positions*. Paris: Minuit, 1972.

DERRIDA, Jacques. 'Semiology and Grammatology' in *Positions* (Alan Bass trans.). Chicago, IL: University of Chicago Press, 1982.

ECO, Umberto. *Dire presque la même chose*. Paris: Grasset, 2006.

FOUCAULT, Michel. 'Nietzsche, Freud, Marx' in *Cahiers de Royaumont*, vol. 4: *Nietzsche*. Paris: Minuit, 1967.

HEIDEGGER, Martin. *Cahier Heidegger*. Paris: L'Herne, 1983.

HEIDEGGER, Martin. 'A Dialogue on Language' in *On the Way to Language* (Peter D. Hertz trans.). New York: Perennial, 1971.

HEIDEGGER, Martin. 'Anaximander's Saying' in *Off the Beaten Track* (Julian Young and Kenneth Haynes eds and trans.). Cambridge: Cambridge University Press, 2002.

HEIDEGGER, Martin. 'Dépassement de la métaphysique' in *Essais et conférences*. Paris: Gallimard, 1997.

HEIDEGGER, Martin. *Heraclitus* (Julia Goesser Assaiante and S. Montgomery Ewegen trans.). New York: Bloomsbury, 2018.

HEIDEGGER, Martin. *Heraklit, Gesamtausgabe*, vol. 55. Frankfurt am Main: Vittorio Klostermann, 1979.

HEIDEGGER, Martin. 'La parole d'Anaximandre' in *Chemins qui ne mènent nulle part*. Paris: Gallimard, 1986.

HEIDEGGER, Martin. 'Letter on "Humanism"' (1946) (Frank A. Capuzzi trans.) in *Pathmarks* (William McNeil ed.). Cambridge: Cambridge University Press, 1998.

HEIDEGGER, Martin. ' . . . L'homme habite en poète . . . ' in *Essais et conférences*. Paris: Gallimard, 1997.

HEIDEGGER, Martin. *Questions I et II*. Paris: Gallimard, 1990.

HUSSEIN, Taha. *Fī alshiʿr aljāhilī, alkitāb alʿawwal*. Cairo: Almaktaba almiṣriya, 1926.

IBN MANZUR. *Lisān al-ʿArab*. Beirut: Dar Sadir, 1955–56.

IBN RUSHD. *Kitāb al-Shiʿr* in *Kitāb Arisṭūṭālīs fī fann al-shiʿr* (Abderrahmane Badawi trans.). Beirut: Dār al-Thaqāfa, 1973.

KILITO, Abdelfattah. *Lan tatakallam lughatī*. Beirut: Dar aṭṭali'a, 2002.

KILITO, Abdelfattah. *Min shurfat Ibn Rushd*. Casablanca: Dār Tūbqāl lil-Nashr, 2009.

LAROUI, Abdallah. *Al-ʾĪdiyūlūjiyā al-ʿarabiyya al-muʿāṣira*. Casablanca: al-Markaz al-Thaqāfī al-ʿArabī, 1995.

LAROUI, Abdallah. *Al-ʾĪdiyūlūjiyā al-ʿarabiyya al-muʿāṣira* (Mohamed Itani trans.). Beirut: Dar al-Ḥaqīqa, 1970.

LAROUI, Abdallah. *Khawāṭir aṣ-ṣabāḥ (1967–1973)*. Casablanca/Beirut: Arab Cultural Centre, 2001.

LAROUI, Abdallah. *L'idéologie arabe contemporaine* (Maxime Rodinson pref.). Paris: F. Maspero, 1967.

Le Monde, 17 December 1993.

MOUBARAK, Zaki. *Al-Akhlāq ʿinda al-Ghazālī*. Cairo: Hindawi Foundation, 1924.

PROUST, Marcel. 'Préface de Bernard de Fallois' in *Contre Sainte-Beuve*. Paris: Gallimard, 1954.

SCHLEGEL, Friedrich. 'Athenaeum Fragments' in *Philosophical Fragments* (Peter Firchow trans.). Minneapolis, MN: University of Minnesota Press, 1991.

SCHLEGEL, Friedrich. 'Fragment de L'Athenaeum' (229) in Philippe Lacoue-Labarthe and Jean-Luc Nancy, *L'Absolu littéraire*. Paris: Éditions du Seuil, 1978.

STRICH, Fritz. *Goethe und die Weltliteratur*. Bern: Franck Verlag, 1946.